the SELF-SABOTAGE behavior workbook

A STEP-BY-STEP PROGRAM TO CONQUER NEGATIVE THOUGHTS, BOOST CONFIDENCE, AND LEARN TO BELIEVE IN YOURSELF

Dr. Candice Seti, PsyD

ULYSSES PRESS

Published in the US by:
Ulysses Press
PO Box 3440
Berkeley, CA 94703
www.ulyssespress.com

ISBN: 978-1-64604-132-9
Library of Congress Control Number: 2020947029

Printed in the United States by Kingery Printing Company
10 9 8 7 6 5 4 3 2 1

Acquisitions editor: Ashten Evans
Managing editor: Claire Chun
Editor: Ariel Adams
Proofreader: Renee Rutledge
Front cover design: Justin Shirley
Interior design: what!design @ whatweb.com
Layout: Jake Flaherty

Contents

PREFACE

Welcome, and congratulations on taking the first step to becoming a sabotage-fighting warrior! You are about to embark upon a journey that has the potential to change your life, build your confidence, and allow you to achieve your dreams. I've written this book as a clinical psychologist, but also as a reformed self-saboteur. I've personally struggled with being a procrastinator, a self-attacker, and an avoider (things we will discuss in depth later!) and have worked with hundreds of individuals who have struggled with their own forms of self-sabotage. In other words, I bring a lot of expertise and a lot of real-world experience to this program, and that is why I am confident that it can help you finally free yourself from the self-sabotage that's keeping you stuck in your life.

Before getting into the substance of the program, it's important to understand what this program is and isn't. This program is a collection of tools and skills that I have gathered together for the express purpose of helping you end your self-sabotage—the way in which you stop yourself from being happy and achieving your goals. This program reflects years of education, clinical experience, and my own firsthand knowledge of what it takes to overcome self-sabotaging tendencies. My approach combines cognitive behavioral therapy, self-care, and paying close attention to your self-talk into a single program that you can work through at your own pace.

This book is also quite interactive. Most chapters will have you engaging in brainstorming activities or creating action plans. As such, most chapters will include worksheets. (Look for the green check mark to let you know you have an assignment.) If you are a pen-and-paper kind of person, you can write directly in the book or make photocopies. If you prefer to work on your computer or tablet, you can download all the worksheets in one workbook directly from www.selfsabotageworkbook.com.

The bottom line is that this program is designed to help you finally get out of your own way—a goal that is so elusive for so many people. It wouldn't surprise me if other parts of your life also get better when you rid yourself of self-sabotage, but don't count on this program to be a panacea. Other problems may need other solutions. Along those lines, it is important to be very clear that this book does not replace medical care by the appropriate professionals. As you work through this book, keep in mind that it is not a medical manual. It is an account of one approach to ending self-sabotaging behaviors. None of the individuals involved in writing, editing, producing, or publishing this book are rendering professional services to the individual reader.

Phew, now that we have that out of the way, let's look at the program.

Chapter 1

INTRODUCTION

"As I look at my life, I might ask, 'Who is the person that represents the greatest threat to me?' And if I happen to have a mirror around somewhere, I can rather quickly answer that question."

—Craig D. Lounsbrough

You have a voice in your head.

No, you are not crazy. You don't have multiple personality disorder. You're not schizophrenic. You don't need to check into a psych ward. You are a normal, healthy, functioning individual just like most of the rest of us. And yet, you still have a voice in your head (as does everyone else.) And unfortunately, that voice is out to get you—to stand in your way, to prevent you from achieving your goals and dreams, and to provide every reason *not* to do what you want to do. That voice is your self-sabotage.

What is self-sabotage?

The answer probably depends on whom you ask. If we look at Webster's definition of sabotage, it is "an act or process tending to hamper or hurt." Now think about that behavior being something you do *to yourself*, and you have a good idea of what I am talking about here. Urban Dictionary defines self-sabotaging as "one who keeps screwing things up for themselves. Usually not on purpose."

I like to think of self-sabotage as simply standing in your own way. In other words, you are blocking yourself from moving forward from the past or achieving whatever it is you want to do in life—finding a romantic relationship, getting a promotion, losing weight, traveling, or doing anything else that you find worth pursuing.

Sounds silly, right? If you want something, why would you stand in the way of achieving it? Why wouldn't you just go and get it? But unfortunately, the human mind is not that simple. In fact, it is as far from straightforward as you can get. We don't think from point A to point B most of the time, so sometimes we do things that are against our own interests. The human mind, and our thoughts and behaviors, are so complex that hundreds of thousands of people have devoted their lives to studying them. The only definite answer when it comes to human behavior is that there aren't any definite answers!

Back to self-sabotage. We can agree that it sounds like a silly thing to do, but we *all* do it! You do it. How do I know? Well, you're reading this book, so I'm assuming you're looking for a way to stop this problem. Also, I know because, as I said above, the human mind isn't as logical and easy to understand as we might believe. Yes, every last one of us self-sabotages, no matter how intelligent we may be.

It's easy to look at someone who's achieved success and say he or she doesn't self-sabotage. For example, let's look at Ted. He's been happily married for 15 years and has two delightful children, aged 9 and 6 years old. He's a director at a large tech company and can easily support his family with his salary. He seems generally happy and well adjusted. On the surface, you would assume that he is someone who simply does not engage in self-sabotage. After all, he couldn't have gotten to this happy, successful place in his life if he stood in his own way all the time, right?

But what if I told you that Ted has had the opportunity to apply for a vice-president job on three different occasions, and each time he failed to submit the necessary documents to be considered for the position? What if I also told you that he and his wife have been struggling for a few years now because she is constantly hassling him to actually finish the things he says he's going to do around the house? And what if I told you that he has about $120,000 in credit card debt? Would these bits of information change your mind about him? Does he suddenly seem like someone you can relate to a bit more? Have you done similar things?

Some of us self-sabotage more frequently than others, and some of us sabotage ourselves in a way that is more debilitating, but we all do it. Actually, it's not a question of *if* we self-sabotage; the better question is how we respond to it and whether or not we fight it. Self-sabotage compounds itself and gets stronger and stronger if we don't stop it in its tracks and push it away. It's usually the *hows* and the *how oftens* of self-sabotage that differentiate successful people from those who are stuck. That's what this program is going to help you tackle.

When I talk to my clients about self-sabotage, every one of them will nod their head and say, "yes, I absolutely do that!" but when I ask them how or ask them to give me examples, they often have to pause to think about it. That's because in order to know how you self-sabotage, you also have to know what you want. If you can't pinpoint exactly what you want, you can't see how self-sabotage stands in your way of getting there. In fact, self-sabotage is often the *only* thing standing in the way of achieving what you want. So, in order to clearly understand your self-sabotage, you also need to clearly understand what you want. Don't worry: we will figure all that out together!

Chapter 2

SELF-SABOTAGE: WHAT YOU NEED TO KNOW

"Self-sabotage is when we say we want something and then go about making sure it doesn't happen."

—Alyce Cornyn-Selby

Every one of us sabotages ourself at one point or another.

Reading that sentence might have made you laugh in disbelief. *Everyone*? Yes, everyone. Even that person who runs a successful business while raising a family. Even that person who lost fifty pounds and has kept it off for years. Even that person who's happily married to the love of their life.

That business owner might be telling herself that she should be satisfied with what she has, so she shouldn't strive for more because she'll never achieve it. The person who lost all that weight might have lost and regained pounds countless times before they reached their goals. The person married to their soulmate probably threw previous relationships away because they were scared to commit.

You were probably drawn to this book because you're tired of standing in your own way and seeing everyone else have the success you crave. You might even feel like there's something wrong with you.

After all, why would you stop *yourself* from getting what you really want? There's nothing wrong with you, and you're not alone. Self-sabotage goes hand in hand with most of the goals people have in their lives, from their careers to their relationships and everything in between.

It can seem fairly harmless at first glance—just a stray thought that stops you from reaching out to a potential connection on LinkedIn, or another thought that tells you that you can watch just one more episode of a show instead of working on the novel you've been trying to write. But it can gradually develop into much more than that, cutting you off from your true potential and causing depression, anxiety, and much more.

Another reason why recognizing self-sabotage can be elusive is that it can masquerade as logic. We might turn ideas over in our head again and again until we talk ourselves out of them with what we think is very good reasoning. Because we think it's a rational and appropriate decision, we don't consciously understand how damaging it is.

Take a job listing, for example. At first glance, it looks like your dream job but, before you know it, you're telling yourself that someone else is more qualified and that now isn't the time to make a career change. You close the tab and move on with your day. Does that sound like a familiar train of thought?

At face value, the words sound somewhat reasonable. You really might be less qualified than someone else, and a career shift might be a little difficult right now. But not even applying is just another way in which you're stopping yourself from opening up to possibilities and getting what you want.

Once you see self-sabotage for what it really is, you can't *un*-see it. It's at home. It's at work. It prevents people from finding true satisfaction in their lives.

And, most important, it's more common than you would think. Psychologist and author Joseph Ferrari suggests that around 20% of Americans procrastinate chronically, meaning it touches every single aspect of their life—from home to work to relationships.[1]

Another survey showed that an astonishing 88% of people in the workforce procrastinate at least one hour a day, if not more. Those extra hours add up.[2] Imagine what you could get done in those hours and how different the world could be if everyone harnessed that extra time toward whatever they were passionate about!

Young people tend to self-sabotage more than older people, and the impact is profound. A 2007 study found that 80 to 90% of college students regularly procrastinated on their coursework, likely producing work below their potential to make their deadlines. In an even more serious example, a

---

1   Kenda Cherry, "What Is Procrastination?" last modified May 30, 2020, https://www.verywellmind.com/the-psychology-of-procrastination-2795944.

2   Darius Foroux, "How Common Is Procrastination? Study," last modified July 4, 2019, https://medium.com/darius-foroux/how-common-is-procrastination-a-study-80869467c3f3.

1997 survey found that procrastination was one of the biggest reasons why PhD candidates didn't complete their dissertations.

Overthinking is another significant element of self-sabotage (and a self-sabotage style we will discuss later), which also seems to impact younger people more than their older counterparts. Of 25- to 35-year-olds, 73% were found to overthink, while only 20% of 65- to 75-year-olds were found to do the same.[3] Overthinking doesn't just contribute to self-sabotage and stop you from getting to your goals. It's a major contributor to severe depression, anxiety, and impaired problem-solving—all things that can snowball into more and more self-sabotage, especially for women.

Women overall tend to be more prone to self-sabotage. Nearly 60% of women are paralyzed by overthinking in comparison to 43% of men, and one in seven admit to criticizing or berating themselves regularly.[4] Some of those women even get their self-criticism in before breakfast, talking down to themselves about their weight, appearance, relationships, or career.[5] You can only imagine how this must set the tone for the day.

Much of this self-criticism can be brushed off as perfectionism (yet another self-sabotage style we will discuss soon). "Perfect" never comes. Perfectionists will either miss out on opportunities because they aren't exactly right, or throw away all their efforts if they make just one mistake. This is especially true for people considered gifted—up to 80% of gifted people would consider themselves perfectionists.[6]

As you can see, there's no group that isn't touched by self-sabotage in one way or another. It's such a common issue, but few people understand how self-sabotage works in their minds and, ultimately, their lives. To understand how to defeat it, you have to study it and understand it, inside and out.

These checkmarks ✔️ throughout the workbook indicate worksheet assignments.
For this first part, use the worksheet on page 10 to write a little bit about your
perspective on your own self-sabotage.

---

3   The Regents of the University of Michigan, "Most Women Think Too Much, Overthinkers Often Drink Too Much," last modified February 4, 2003, http://ns.umich.edu/Releases/2003/Feb03/r020403c.html.

4   The Regents of the University of Michigan, "Most Women Think Too Much."

5   Angela Laguipo, "Average Woman Criticizes Self Eight Times a Day: A Study," last modified January 6, 2016. https://www.techtimes.com/articles/121454/20160106/average-woman-criticizes-self-eight-times-a-day-study.htm.

6   Lisa Natcharian, "Real Learning: Meet the Perfectionists," last modified March 25, 2019, https://www.masslive.com/real_learning/2010/07/meet_the_perfectionists.html.

✔How I See Myself Engaging in Self-Sabotage

Write some first thoughts about your self-sabotaging behaviors: how they occur in your life; how you think you do it; what goals you see yourself sabotaging:

_____

_____

_____

_____

_____

_____

_____

_____

_____

_____

_____

_____

_____

_____

_____

_____

_____

_____

SECTION 1

How We Do It

Chapter 3

CREATING SELF-FULFILLING PROPHECIES

"The only reason I can't jump in and engage life is that I've told myself I can't. Yet I can't help wondering would happen if I told myself I could?"

—Craig D. Lounsbrough

We now know that none of us are immune to self-sabotage, even if everything appears fine from the outside. Though it's important to realize that self-sabotage happens to everyone, it's ultimately not about who does it and how frequently. It's really about *how* we do it. After all, you wouldn't try to fix any problem without understanding what it looks like and how it affects you.

Let's look at the different types of self-saboteurs to help you to more clearly define what your own self-sabotage looks like. As we go through these profiles, you most likely will not fall into just one category. Most of us have several different forms of self-sabotage depending on the situation. For instance, you might be a Procrastinator at work, but an Overthinker at home. So don't feel like you need to force yourself into just one category.

Within the worlds of self-sabotage, we hold ourselves back in many different ways and create many different outcomes for ourselves. Let's first look at the sabotage category of those who set up self-fulfilling prophecies—The Procrastinator, The Overthinker, and The Assumer:

THE PROCRASTINATOR

Jessica is assigned a big presentation for work, due in two weeks. It's not only a lot of work, but it's a lot of pressure. If she does a great job, she'll be a shoo-in for the promotion she's been eyeing. The role offers a big increase in pay, and the responsibilities are more in line with what Jessica wants to do. It's the perfect step toward what she wants in her career.

She tells herself that she'll start on it tomorrow.

But she doesn't. Then the day after that, she decides to rewatch her favorite TV show all night. And the days after that, she reorganizes her already-tidy closet, goes out for drinks with her friends, and scrolls through Instagram until two in the morning.

Before she knows it, the two weeks she had for preparation have become three days. She spends those three days rushing through the work, trying to get the bare minimum done so she doesn't show up empty handed.

After she finishes her presentation, she wants to kick herself. She knows she didn't do nearly as good a job as she could have. Why did she put it off so long if getting this promotion meant so much to her?

Does that sound like someone you can relate to? The Procrastinator is the most well-known self-saboteur, especially with all the distraction opportunities that exist today, right at our fingertips. But many of us will describe ourselves as procrastinators without understanding that it isn't just a matter of putting something off—it's a way we sabotage ourselves.

We use phrases like "I work better under pressure" or "I perform better with a time crunch," but these statements are really excuses to continue our sabotaging behavior. The reality is that a lot of procrastinators get things done, but at the last possible minute, making it easier to fall back on the excuse that at least you aren't missing deadlines.

If you're getting things done (albeit at the last minute), you might be asking, how is procrastination a form of self-sabotage? Well, procrastination is delay, which is the manifestation of putting off until tomorrow what you can do today. That can have a lot of negative outcomes:

➡️ **It wastes time or creates unproductive time.** Few people procrastinate by tackling other equally important or pressing projects. Usually, they're watching TV, playing video games, scrolling through social media, and generally avoiding anything that takes much effort. Whether you realize it or not, this is shaping your self-perspective. If you spend a lot of time doing unproductive things, the feeling of not being productive will affect everything in your life. So you will internalize the idea that you're not a productive person, which impacts your overall drive and your confidence moving forward.

➡️ **It sets you up to believe you can only achieve by putting things off.** If you procrastinate because you "work well under pressure" or "need that intense time crunch," you start to believe this is the ONLY way you can achieve. This behavior ultimately reinforces itself, making the idea of doing something ahead of time unfathomable. You start to believe you can't produce without making all projects time sensitive by putting them off. Once you believe this, your conviction that there's no other way to do things solidifies.

➡️ **It never lets you get ahead.** When you live by procrastination's rules, you tend to always do the bare minimum. Why? Because you haven't given yourself enough time to do more. Let's go back to Jessica's presentation. She had two weeks to put together her work, yet she finished it in the nick of time. Imagine if she had started working on it right away. She would have had the rest of the week to review it, add to it, insert charts and diagrams, build on her ideas and concepts, and more. This would push the bar further and make her presentation truly shine, which could have gotten her the promotion she wanted. But her procrastination kept her—and keeps you—from improving and getting ahead.

THE OVERTHINKER

Mary has a third date with a man she's really attracted to so, needless to say, she's excited. She takes the afternoon off from work so she can get her hair done, pick out the right outfit, and prepare. But just as she's about to leave the house, her date texts her and says he's caught up at work and can't make it.

Mary is crushed. Is he really at work? Or is he just trying to get out of their date?

She thinks back to their last date, which ended with a kiss. Was the kiss bad? Had she done something that turned him off? That must be it. She knew he was faking a smile when he said goodbye, and he hadn't been texting back as quickly as he had before. He must be trying to let her down easy.

By the time they reschedule, Mary is convinced that he's just humoring her, so she cancels the date. She thinks she's unattractive and unworthy of love.

The Overthinker is the person who thinks everything to death, often in a way that puts extreme emphasis on the negative. If The Overthinker is asked to do something, instead of just doing it, they think through every aspect of why they were asked to do it and what the potential outcomes are. Even something small, like being invited to a party, can turn into a spiral of anxious thoughts.

Because their thinking tends to be negative, this overthinking leads them to believe they were asked to do something for negative reasons or that the outcome will be bad no matter what. Since they interpret most situations in an unfavorable light, Overthinkers read way too much into others' behaviors, assuming what the other person is feeling.

If you're an Overthinker, if someone is short with you, for instance, you think *you* are unattractive or unpleasant to be around. The idea of that person having a bad day wouldn't even cross your mind. If your significant other reschedules a date or doesn't text you back within a certain amount of time, it's not because they're too busy—it's because you've done something wrong or you are unlovable. Ultimately, as an Overthinker, you take other people's behavior personally and you spend too much time in your own head instead of in your actual interactions.

How does this sabotage you?

➡ **It strips your confidence and creates constant self-doubt.** The Overthinker often sees the behavior of others as being about themselves. Because these thoughts can never be proven right or wrong, The Overthinker always assumes they're right. And because these thoughts often have a negative slant, The Overthinker starts to feel self-conscious and to question their own value or self-worth in every single interaction they have, even if it seems positive from an objective perspective.

➡ **It overfocuses you on the negative and sets up a self-fulfilling prophecy.** As with other self-sabotage styles, overthinking can definitely create a self-fulfilling prophecy. Because The Overthinker tends to act based on their worst fears or thoughts, they never get an opportunity to decide whether or not their thoughts were accurate. For instance, they might assume someone hates them after having just one conversation, and miss out on making a new friend. Like The Assumer, they set themselves up to believe they were correct in thinking the worst of any situation, which reinforces the drive to continually focus on the negative.

➡ **It forces you to need control and certainty.** Since The Overthinker assumes the true meaning behind people's actions, they often feel the need to influence or control what others do in order to feel secure. For instance, if your friend cancels on you, you might repeatedly ask them if they're mad at you, just to feel secure, even if it irritates your friend. Since most things in life aren't certain, The Overthinker may bulldoze over people's boundaries to relieve their own fears.

THE ASSUMER

John has recently gone through a breakup, so his friend invites him to a party, thinking it'll be a great way for him to get back out there. John isn't much of a party person, so the idea of going to one to "get back out there" is extremely unappealing. He knows he won't have any fun and he doubts he'll meet anyone new. And even if he does, he knows that inevitably, the relationship will go sour like his last one did.

He skips out on the party and plays video games all night instead.

You know what they say about assuming, right? The Assumer is someone who's always predicting the future and acting on those predictions before seeing if they come true. They decide how they are going to feel, what is going to happen, and how people are going to react, before even entering into a situation. And in all these cases, they assume that the outcome will be negative.

The Assumer often thinks or says things like, "I'm not going to have fun so there's no point in going," "I'm never going to succeed so why bother trying," and "They are not going to like my ideas so I'm just not going to say anything." Because they think they can clearly see the future, The Assumer tends to talk themself out of most behaviors that would move them forward. If you are an Assumer, this habit sabotages you in numerous ways:

➡ **It prevents you from taking action and keeps you stuck.** By assuming you won't succeed, or you won't have fun, or you won't be liked, you avoid anxiety-provoking situations and never act on the possibility that you might be wrong. As such, you end up stuck in your present situation, just as unhappy as you assume you would be if you went to that party or talked to that person you're interested in.

➡ **It closes you off to new opportunities.** By deciding what is going to happen before it happens, you stop yourself from taking any chances. Going back to the example of John, he assumed that he wouldn't meet anyone he was interested in at the party. He might not have met someone he'd want to date, but he might have met someone he could network with or have as a friend. By assuming that the outcome would be negative, he closed himself off to many positive opportunities to grow.

➡️ **It never allows you to prove yourself wrong.** By deciding there is going to be a negative outcome if you try something, you end up not doing that thing, and you ultimately reinforce your beliefs that nothing good comes from trying anything new. You're left with your thoughts and ideas of what could happen, which can't be disproved. By never going through with anything, you never allow yourself the opportunity to prove your assumptions wrong.

> Do you create self-fulfilling prophecies through your self-sabotage?
> Take the quiz on page 19 to find out if this is your self-sabotage style.

✔Do I Create Self-Fulfilling Prophecies?

Take the quiz to find out if this is your self-sabotage style. For each statement that describes you, circle the Y to the right.

I'm not good at working without a time crunch.	Y		
I often think things to death.		Y	
I'm often sure I know what the outcome of a situation is going to be.			Y
I often find myself leaving things to the last minute.	Y		
I spend a lot of time stuck in my head.		Y	
I know how people feel about me without them telling me.			Y
Most of my day feels unproductive.	Y		
I replay conversations in my head a lot after the fact.		Y	
I know what things I will enjoy and not enjoy without having to try them.			Y
I rarely make arrangements or plans ahead of time.	Y		
I often rehearse what I'm going to say.		Y	
I don't enjoy new places or experiences.			Y
I tend to put off making decisions.	Y		
I'm not very spontaneous.		Y	
I can talk myself out of a lot.			Y
I often say, "I'll do it tomorrow."	Y		
I have trouble sleeping because I can't stop my head from spinning.		Y	
I know when friends/family are upset with me without them telling me.			Y
I have a lot of to-dos that never get done.	Y		
I often worry about why someone hasn't responded to a text or email.		Y	
I often expect the worst.			Y
I rarely get things done ahead of time.	Y		
I often don't believe compliments given to me are genuine.		Y	
I don't take a lot of risks.			Y
Total			

Add up each column. Over 4 suggests a tendency toward creating self-fulfilling prophecies.
Column 1 = Procrastinator. 2 = Overthinker. 3 = Assumer.

Chapter 4

REMOVING POSITIVES FROM OUR LIVES

"Resistance by definition is self-sabotage."

—Steven Pressfield

Self-sabotage doesn't always look like avoiding the things that will get you where you want to go. Some self-saboteurs, instead of thinking their way out of things, putting something off, or looking at their future in a negative light, can actively go out of their way to remove positive things from their life.

You're probably asking yourself how this kind of self-sabotage works. Wouldn't someone who falls into these categories eventually catch on to how they're standing in their own way? Again, you have to understand how this kind of self-sabotage can sneak into your life without your even noticing. Let's look at three kinds of self-saboteur who remove positive things from their life: The Avoider, The Self-Protector, and The Control Freak.

THE AVOIDER

Sasha's best friend wins an all-expenses-paid trip to Hawaii and invites Sasha along. Sasha never imagined she would have the opportunity to go to Hawaii, and the idea of going with all expenses paid sounds too good to be true.

And yet, she hesitates. Hawaii looks beautiful, but what if it's not everything it's cracked up to be? And it's so far, too. Anything could happen, and she'd be too far away from her family to do anything about it. Plus, you wouldn't go to Hawaii without going to the beach. The idea of putting on a swimsuit and having her picture taken, especially after having a baby a year ago, makes Sasha want to run and hide.

Sasha texts her best friend and tells her that she can't go, claiming that she can't be away from her family that long.

The Avoider is a classic self-saboteur who simply avoids situations that cause them anxiety or push them out of their comfort zone. For instance, an Avoider might be uncomfortable in social situations, so they regularly turn down invitations to parties or gatherings. Maybe they're fearful of new situations, so they avoid travel or exposure to new environments, like Sasha in the example above. Maybe they lack confidence at work, so they don't speak up or share ideas.

If you are an Avoider, can you see how this behavior sabotages your success and your life goals?

➡ **It limits growth opportunities.** This one seems pretty obvious: how can you expose yourself to growth opportunities when you avoid everything? Growth opportunities often exist slightly outside of your comfort zone and, as an Avoider, you structure your life in such a way that you rarely venture out of that comfortable place. In the end, you are sacrificing growth to stay comfortable, even if you truly want to make a change in your life.

➡ **It reinforces fears.** The Avoider lives in fear of everything outside of their bubble and retreats into their comfort zone to stay safe from whatever scares them, whether it's standing out in a crowd, getting close to people, or doing something new. If you are staying safe in this way, you reinforce the idea that everything you are avoiding is dangerous and everything you are doing is "the right thing" to keep you safe and protected. Since you avoid everything, there's no counterargument to show that branching out can be a good thing.

➡ **It removes positive and enjoyable opportunities and experiences from life.** Joyful opportunities and leisure activities are things that, as an Avoider, you will usually miss out on. You will tend to say no to possibilities that most of us would consider fun or positive since they aren't the norm. Because these opportunities are outside of your regular routine, you determine that they're dangerous and opt to do nothing instead of something.

THE SELF-PROTECTOR

When Wilma tells her best friends about the new guy she's been seeing for the past few months, they're thrilled for her. But Wilma's feelings aren't so straightforward. This guy seems perfect—he's attractive, funny, considerate, and passionate about his career.

But that's the problem—maybe things are *too* perfect. Someone this funny, considerate, and passionate will likely get bored with her and, if she lets herself get attached, she believes she's setting herself up to get seriously hurt. It's happened before, and she definitely doesn't want to experience that kind of pain again.

Wilma cancels their next date and eventually breaks it off with him, right when her guy suggests that they make their relationship more serious.

The Self-Protector is someone who's constantly covered in metaphorical armor. They're always on the defense and keep their guard up because they believe an attack could be coming around any corner. The Self-Protector essentially lives in fear of ever getting hurt, so they set up a fortress around themselves. This often means keeping all relationships at a distance, never getting close enough to people to let them hurt you and never allowing yourself to be vulnerable. How exactly does this fall into the category of self-sabotage?

➡ **Your romantic relationships never have any real depth, emotionality, or in many cases, longevity.** Romantic relationships are often the riskiest relationships for The Self-Protector. You may have been hurt once in the past and as a result, live in fear of it ever happening again. So you keep romantic relationships at bay simply by never having relationships last very long or by always keeping relationships casual, or keeping your significant other at arm's length. This only reinforces your fear of getting hurt, since your relationships are constantly ending.

➡ **You miss out on the benefits of deeper relationships.** Friendships and relationships with family members are also scary to The Self-Protector. You might have very few friends and may not be very close with members of your family in fear that they'll cause problems in your life instead of adding joy to it. It may be a fear of issues arising, or of losing the relationship in one way or another and getting hurt as a result. Because you keep everyone fairly distant, you don't get to experience all the positives of having a close relationship: warmth, trust, connection, intimacy, compassion, and more.

➡ **You don't ever allow yourself to be truly vulnerable.** By being afraid of getting hurt, you never feel truly safe with anyone and never let your guard down. You never let yourself be vulnerable, never truly opening yourself or your heart up completely. Since you aren't showing the deepest parts of yourself, you are never truly seen, understood, or loved on a meaningful level.

THE CONTROL FREAK

Angela's daughter has recently started her first year of high school, which means she has new friends. Angela wants her to be social, but she's also terrified that her daughter will start to distance herself from her. They've always been close, and Angela doesn't want to lose that relationship.

So she tries her best to keep her daughter under control, even if she's not physically there. She checks all of her daughter's texts every night to make sure that she's not getting into trouble, insists on coming along with her and her friends to the movies, and doesn't allow her to go to the school dance with the boy she really likes.

Angela ends up pushing her daughter away—her daughter, who wants to have some independence, tells her she's too controlling.

The Control Freak likes to ensure that they are never surprised or caught off guard. They want to be prepared for every situation and interaction, and their method of doing that is to control everything they possibly can. As a result, they tend to avoid situations where they're less likely to have control, and they often become fearful of these situations. Angela feared that she and her daughter would drift apart, so she tried to control whom her daughter talked to and how she interacted with her friends, and her approach ultimately backfired.

Control Freaks tend to overpower those around them, and they don't like to put themselves at risk. This type of self-sabotage is very similar to that of The Avoider in that it reinforces anxieties and holds you back from positive things. Here's how this kind of self-sabotage can hold you back:

➡ **It limits growth opportunities.** Because you are always in control of your environment and your situation, you'll rarely encounter something new. If it's new, it's risky and might lead to an outcome that scares you. It also limits opportunities that other people give you, since they're also not entirely within your control.

➡ **It reinforces your anxiety.** By always keeping a firm grip on your environment and your situation, you start to believe that having control is the only way to be safe. As your controlling tendencies continue and no threats present themselves, you constantly reinforce your belief that threats exist when you are not in control.

➡ **It limits your social engagements and social opportunities.** By always needing to be in control, you end up controlling those around you and the situations that you engage in socially. In Angela's case, she tried to control her daughter's social life in an attempt to keep her daughter close. This means people who have more dominant personalities or those who might create new opportunities for you are less likely to stay in your social circle—they'll know that you won't want to try anything new or that you'll dilute whatever opportunity they're offering so it's easier for you to stomach.

Take the quiz on page 26 to see if you remove positives from your life.

✔ Do I Remove Positives from My Life?

Take the quiz to find out if this is your self-sabotage style. For each statement that describes you, circle the Y to the right.

I don't get out much.	Y		
Relationships often feel scary.		Y	
I don't like surprises.			Y
I don't cry in front of people.		Y	
I'm usually the planner.			Y
My life is pretty repetitive.	Y		
I have acquaintances but not a lot of close friends.		Y	
I'm a nervous car passenger.			Y
There's not a huge amount of excitement in my life.	Y		
I rarely let my guard down.		Y	
I have a hard time admitting I was wrong.			Y
I would consider myself an introvert.	Y		
I'm not very close with my family.		Y	
I rarely ask for help.			Y
I don't take a lot of risks.	Y		
I've been hurt before and want to avoid that ever happening again.		Y	
I like to keep my personal environment organized.			Y
I turn down a lot of invitations.	Y		
I don't open up about my feelings a lot.		Y	
I like to be prepared in most situations.			Y
I'm happy to stay at home most of the time.	Y		
I worry about losing people.		Y	
I don't like depending on others.			Y
Total			

Add up each column. Over 4 suggests a tendency toward removing positives.

Column 1 = Avoider. 2 = Self-Protector. 3 = Control Freak.

Chapter 5

LOWERING OUR SELF-WORTH

"Much of your self-esteem doesn't come from what happens to you on a given day or what somebody says, but what you know about yourself on the inside."

—Dr. Judy Ho

The previous types of self-sabotage mostly involved taking things away: avoiding a potentially uncomfortable situation, talking yourself out of something that could be good for your growth, or pushing away any situation that you couldn't control.

Self-sabotage often takes the opposite approach, piling on heaps of negative actions or thoughts that cheat you out of reaching your goals. Ultimately, this approach lowers your view of yourself in a way similar to that of the avoidant types of self-sabotage—you reinforce the idea that you aren't worthy of getting what you want, which stops you from trying. Let's explore what self-sabotage that lowers your self-worth looks like in three types of self-saboteur: The Overindulger, The Self-Critic, and The Perfectionist.

THE OVERINDULGER

> Nina is finally down twenty pounds. She's stuck to her diet and never missed a workout, and now she feels better than she has in quite a while. Her sister's wedding is coming up, and she has a plan to stay on track, even during the festivities.
>
> But then, she gets offered an unplanned slice of cake. That turns into two, plus way more champagne than she can handle. The champagne gives her a horrible hangover, which makes her miss spin class. And of course, she decides a greasy ham, egg, and cheese sandwich is the best cure for her hangover. It's the first one she's had in months. The rest of the weekend turns into a feast of all the foods she's missed.
>
> She treats herself to another ham, egg, and cheese on Monday morning, blowing her diet for the rest of the week. She tells herself that she'll get right back onto her diet, stricter than ever, next Monday.

The Overindulger likes to turn a little into a lot. Instead of having one cupcake, they have a weekend binge fest, like Nina in the example above. Instead of having a drink the night before a big interview to calm their nerves, they have seven, which of course leads to problems that are far worse than being nervous.

The Overindulger is lacking in moderation and balance, which means they're either "off" or "on." Nina was on her diet completely, but she used one slip-up as an excuse to get completely off track. Someone who's trying to quit smoking might face a similar situation. One cigarette during a night at the bar? Might as well turn it into half a pack.

Since The Overindulger thinks of things in these terms, they keep themselves stuck or even move themselves backward—the ultimate self-sabotage. You can easily see how it sabotages:

➡ **It prevents you from achieving your goals.** The Overindulger engages in behavior that is detrimental to meeting their goals, no matter how badly they want to. This often becomes a pendulum swing: they set themselves up with too high a goal ("I'm just going to eat chicken and broccoli for three weeks!") and then end up swinging completely in the other direction if they slip up once ("I already had one bite of cake—might as well finish the whole thing"). As a result, they remain stuck in this back-and-forth behavior, unable to maintain balance long enough to make progress.

➡ **It sets you up to believe you have no self-control.** The nature of this extreme behavior creates the perception of lack of control. Overindulgers often set themselves up with extremely high goals, which they ultimately don't reach. Rather than thinking their goals are unrealistic, they believe that they lack the self-control to achieve them; they start to believe that they can't manage any of their options. They ultimately end up not believing in themselves and feeling they are incapable of reaching their goals.

⇒ **It creates an all-or-nothing behavioral loop.** The Overindulger is all about black-and-white thinking and all-or-nothing behavior. They set up goals that they are completely "into," and then, when they deviate even slightly, they are "all out." In Nina's case, she had too much cake and champagne. Instead of getting back on track once she felt better, she went all out on foods she missed.

This back-and-forth yo-yoing ends up transferring to just about every aspect of their life: food, weight, career, relationships, self-esteem, finances, parenting, and more.

THE SELF-CRITIC

Molly loves to write, and finally she has the chance to read her work in front of some writers she really admires. It starts well, with the writers praising her writing style and the story's plot. But then, one writer points out that one of her characters is a bit flat and suggests some ways to enhance the character. When she hears that, all of the praise from the other writers goes out the window.

On her way home, she blames herself—why didn't she focus more on character development before going out with her work? She thinks she'll never make it as a writer. She puts her work in progress aside, feeling too defeated to edit it.

Self-criticism is pretty common. Many of us even present it as humorous, using self-deprecating humor to make others laugh. But Self-Critics are much harsher on themselves in private than they are in public.

The Self-Critic is constantly analyzing their own behavior and beating themselves up for their shortfalls. The Self-Critic tends to ignore evidence that is positive and overemphasize evidence to suggest they are flawed or damaged, just as Molly did in the example. She got positive feedback from writers she truly admired, but none of it mattered because one of them didn't think it was perfect. Also, by taking the feedback as a comment on who she is as a person, she missed out on an opportunity to improve her work.

Being overly self-critical can be a significant form of self-sabotage for many reasons.

➡ **It is completely unmotivating.** It's not uncommon to believe that self-attack and beating ourselves up is a way to change things or push ourselves to be better. But the reality is that it is not even remotely motivating—it's almost always the opposite. We stop wanting to do anything because we know that we're going to beat ourselves up about it, or as a result of all the self-criticism we simply stop believing we are even capable.

Think about it—if you were trying motivate someone else, you wouldn't call them stupid or tell them they're not good enough. They wouldn't want to push themselves, and when you attack yourself, you're doing the same thing.

➡ **It sets you up to have low self-esteem.** Constant criticism from anyone would make us feel bad about ourselves, but when the criticism is coming from within, it's even more damaging. After all, who knows you better than you know yourself? Since you feel you know yourself best, you might believe the criticism is more real than criticism—or praise—from the outside. The buildup of self-criticism gradually makes you feel worse and worse about yourself until your self-esteem hits rock bottom.

➡ **It makes you unwilling to push yourself or branch out.** The constant criticism of yourself leaves you unmotivated and with low self-esteem, as mentioned before. If you're unmotivated and don't believe you're worthwhile anyway, you won't have any drive to push yourself harder, to expose yourself to anything new, or to even find the energy to achieve your existing goals. Without the drive, you lose all ability to propel yourself forward.

THE PERFECTIONIST

Violet wants to get into amazing shape for a trip she's planning to go on in three months, so she hits the gym. She follows countless fitness personalities on Instagram, who have inspired her to make a change. She doesn't miss a single workout, pushes herself as hard as she can, and starts buying clothes a size smaller. The week of the trip rolls around, and she decides to try on the clothes she bought.

The image in the mirror isn't what she thought it would be. She looks smaller and healthier, but she doesn't look the way she wants to, like all of those fitness images on Instagram. She feels like her thighs still look too big and she's not a fan of her waist. She wonders why she even bothered with this whole exercise program.

She quits the gym after her trip—why bother going if she can't get the perfect body?

The Perfectionist can be seen as being very similar to The Self-Critic, but there are some key differences in the way they approach their self-sabotage. The Perfectionist has an ideal in mind for everything; a standard that they are always trying to meet or live up to. In Violet's case, she dreamed of looking like one of the fitness models she saw on Instagram, a body type that very few people have naturally. Violet's standards, and the standards of other perfectionists, are pretty black and white. So any outcome that is not perfect ultimately amounts to being a failure.

With these kinds of standards, success often feels impossible, which sets up The Perfectionist either to give up when they don't meet their own expectations or to not even bother trying. In their world, it is either perfect, or it's nothing at all—there are no gray areas for The Perfectionist. This approach is self-sabotaging in many of the ways we've previously discussed:

➡ **It creates an all-or-nothing behavior loop.** The drive for perfection and only seeing things in black and white terms makes it easy to be either "completely into" or "all-out," just as we saw in The Overindulger. Violet's perfectionism made her focus on the fact that she didn't look exactly like she wanted to rather than noticing all the ways she *had* improved. The Perfectionist often tries things but as soon as they realize that they may not achieve their ideal, they immediately go "all out" and give up.

➡ **It creates avoidance behavior.** Because The Perfectionist has such high standards, they are often unlikely to even attempt something without believing they'll be 100% successful. Since no one gets everything right, even with practice, they end up avoiding doing things all together. This often means avoiding competitions they don't believe they can win, avoiding career advancement opportunities they are unsure of, and avoiding personal tasks that have often lived in their "to-do" list for an eternity.

➡ **It sets them up for self-criticism and self-attack.** The black and white thinking of The Perfectionist creates a lot of avoidance, but it also creates a lot of perceived failure. The Perfectionist tends to beat themself up for not achieving 100% and for not doing what they expect of themself. Like other types of self-saboteurs, they look on the negative side of things rather than seeing what they have actually achieved. As this self-attack continues, their self-esteem rapidly hits rock bottom.

Take the quiz on page 32 to see if you lower your self-worth.

✔Do I Lower My Self-Worth?

Take the quiz to find out if this is your self-sabotage style. For each statement that describes you, circle the Y to the right.

I'm often on and off of diets.	Y		
I tend to make a lot of mistakes.		Y	
I strive for perfection in most things.			Y
I'm an all-or-nothing kind of person.	Y		
I judge myself pretty harshly.		Y	
I don't like things that I'm not good at.			Y
I don't believe in doing anything halfway.	Y		
My sense of humor is pretty self-deprecating.		Y	
I'm not very good at delegating.			Y
I have an addictive personality.	Y		
I have body image issues.		Y	
I have a hard time being happy for others' successes.			Y
I'm not good at moderation.	Y		
I don't compliment myself or accept compliments well.		Y	
I'm afraid of getting criticized for mistakes I make.			Y
I like to set high goals for myself.	Y		
I don't forgive easily.		Y	
Failing at something makes me feel like a failure as a person.			Y
When I want something, I'm laser-focused on it.	Y		
I don't have very good self-esteem.		Y	
I can spend thirty minutes writing and rewriting a brief email.			Y
I don't have a lot of self-control.	Y		
I tend to beat myself up for things I've done wrong.		Y	
I fixate on mistakes I've made.			Y
Total			

Add up each column. Over 4 suggests a tendency toward lowering self-worth.

Column 1 = Overindulger. 2 = Self-Critic. 3 = Perfectionist.

Chapter 6

WHY IT'S A BIG DEAL

"People who self-handicap purposely shoot themselves in the foot in order to protect themselves from having to confront their possible shortcomings. Many self-handicapping behaviors are those small, subtle bad habits like being late, gossiping, micromanaging, behaving passive-aggressively, or being a perfectionist. We may not recognize these self-defeating—and self-handicapping—traits for what they are. Or we may even wrongly perceive them as strengths. But in truth, they often get in the way of us blooming."

—Rich Karlgaard

You've probably found that you're self-sabotaging in one way or another, and you're probably starting to see how that behavior is holding you back. But is it really that big a deal, especially if so many of the scenarios from the last chapter are common? If *everyone* is self-sabotaging, and many people are clearly hitting their goals, then why should we care?

Self-sabotage can make every single part of your life fall below what you're capable of, meaning you'll often find yourself feeling unsatisfied. In some cases, you can get stuck in cycles that actively destroy your life. Your overall happiness will suffer if you don't acknowledge your self-sabotage and end it before it gets out of control.

Let's start with how significantly self-sabotage can affect your health. Every time January rolls around, people make resolutions to get healthier by eating better, losing weight, starting an exercise program, or quitting smoking. And by the time March rolls around? Nearly all of those people have given up, likely due to self-sabotage.

Nearly 90% of people who lose a significant amount of weight gain it back within a year, and 60 to 90% of people who quit smoking relapse within the first year. If your weight is slightly above average, or your lifestyle isn't perfect but could use a little improvement, self-sabotaging your efforts won't have noticeable immediate implications on your life—but it will be brewing below the surface and setting you up.

And the situation is a bit different for those people with more pressing issues—say those who need to lose significant amounts of weight quickly to cure their diabetes, or quit smoking immediately before they further damage their lungs, or start an exercise program to improve their cardiovascular health in order to reduce their risk of strokes or heart attacks. For these people, self-sabotage can literally mean the difference between life and death.

Even before you're hit by the deadlier consequences of excess weight, lack of fitness, or smoking, self-sabotaging your health can also affect your day-to-day life. Say you're an Overindulger: not only will your whirlwind post-diet binges impact your weight, but afterward you'll probably feel bloated, groggy, and far from your best. If these consequences are combined with any event where you have to be at your best, like a presentation or a date, you've no doubt negatively impacted that as well.

Also, the stress and anxiety that all forms of self-sabotage can bring up can hurt your health, causing high blood pressure, sleep problems, headaches, and more.[7]

Additionally, a lot of stress comes from our relationships, especially our intimate ones. As we covered in the previous chapter, being an Overthinker or a Self-Protector can blow everyday relationship occurrences into something destructive. Canceled plans aren't just canceled plans—they're signs that your partner is cheating on you or isn't committed to you. A nice gift isn't just a loving gesture— it's a sign that you need to end the relationship before it gets too serious and you risk getting hurt.

These self-sabotage patterns lead to fights, jealousy, and tension, which naturally lead to breakups and even divorce. According to the American Psychological Association, about half of US marriages end in divorce—*half*. And according to data collected by WotWentWrong, an app that tracks why people break up, the most common reason why couples who dated more than six months split was "too much fighting."

---

7   Mayo Clinic Staff, "Stress Symptoms." April 4, 2019, https://www.mayoclinic.org/healthy-lifestyle/stress-management/in-depth/stress-symptoms/ art-20050987#:~:text=Indeed%2C%20stress%20symptoms%20can%20affect,heart%20disease%2C%20obesity%20and%20diabetes.

Though many people going through those divorces or breakups didn't realize it, they were likely victims of self-sabotage. This issue, which many people don't even recognize is happening inside their heads, can create some of the most disruptive, painful changes in their lives.

The havoc that self-sabotage can wreak doesn't stop in your relationships. As discussed in the last chapter, self-sabotage can hold you back at work and in your education. Of course, this keeps you stagnant, but if you're making enough money to get by, is it really that bad?

Yes, it can be! Say you're an Assumer who assumes that everyone who's good at public speaking was born with those skills and that you can't improve upon them. In turn, that misbelief stops you from moving into a more prestigious role at work. The idea that you can't change your abilities makes you more anxious and disoriented, which causes your performance to suffer.

Also, a study from the Bureau of Labor Statistics showed that a positive self-image was strongly correlated with better overall career satisfaction, higher pay, and as mentioned earlier, better health. It's not just about getting promotions—it's about doing and feeling your best wherever you are. Self-sabotage can stop you from experiencing that.

Lower performance at work can also lead to money troubles, as does self-sabotage in managing day-to-day finances. Of course, if you think that you aren't worthy of a promotion, your salary won't grow. But you can also self-sabotage like an Overindulger who might go on a shopping spree after slipping up on their budget once. Or you may be a Procrastinator and put things off so much that you fail out of college and hurt your chances of getting a higher-paying job.

Another underacknowledged aspect of self-sabotage is how it can lead down the dark path of addiction. Many addictions start as self-sabotage before developing into an even bigger problem. The Procrastinator can use addictive behaviors to push off whatever needs to be done; the Control Freak might use food to make them feel better and give them a sense of control over their own lives.

Let's look at a more detailed example of how these self-sabotage behaviors play out.

Thirty-five-year-old Joey is a classic Avoider who lives alone with his two cats. He works from home, so his apartment is his safe space, his comfort zone. His sister lives nearby, and he's spent enough time at her place to be comfortable there as well, going to dinners at her house once a week.

But other than their two homes, Joey isn't comfortable anywhere. Every time he used to go into a new environment, his anxiety would climb sky high. Now, he's basically stopped going anywhere outside of his bubble. He doesn't socialize with friends, he doesn't date, and he doesn't go to events—all of these activities would be opportunities for him to feel uncomfortable and anxious, so why would he willingly put himself into those situations? He's been living like this, between his apartment and his sister's house, for four years.

Joey has always enjoyed a little bit of alcohol, too. He had been a fairly regular beer drinker for years, having three or four beers a night several nights a week, and as his avoidance behavior got more and more severe, he found himself turning to alcohol more and more frequently. It helped distract him from his loneliness, and it gave him something to do night after night with only his cats for company.

He started drinking tequila several years ago, starting with two tequila drinks a night. He quickly moved on to shots instead of mixed drinks because they took away the loneliness faster, and then he started pairing the shots with beer. Now, he has eight to ten shots of tequila a night with about six beers, and he can't seem to stop.

Joey has developed alcoholism. His behavior is addictive, meaning he no longer has the ability to NOT drink and will choose drinking above other things (even his weekly dinner at his sister's). This behavior started as a simple way to avoid his feelings of isolation and loneliness and slowly developed into an even more severe problem.[8]

Obviously, not all self-sabotage cases are as extreme as Joey's, but they can become so if left unchecked. Joey's addiction, in addition to all the consequences described, illustrate why we need to take self-sabotage seriously. If we don't, our ideal future lives—or our current lives—can crumble away without our even realizing it.

Reading all of this might make you feel hopeless or scared, especially if you see self-sabotage in multiple areas of your life, but don't worry. You have the power to change, and reading this book is a great first step. Taking an active role in stopping self-sabotage will change your life for the better. Let's talk about how to do that.

This is *not* a book on addiction treatment. If you are struggling with alcohol or drug addiction, please call the Substance Abuse and Mental Health Services Administration's National Helpline—1-800-662-HELP (4357).

> As you probably know, self-sabotage is a way that we all hold ourselves back from achieving what we really want and living the life that makes us happy. Use the worksheet on pages 37 to 38 to learn how your self-sabotage is personally holding you back from the life you want.

8   Mayo Clinic Staff, "Stress Symptoms." https://www.mayoclinic.org/healthy-lifestyle/stress-management/in-depth/stress-symptoms/art-20050987

✔ How My Self-Sabotage Is Holding Me Back

What I want in a relationship that I haven't achieved:

_____

_____

What I want in a career that I haven't achieved:

_____

_____

What I want in my friendships/family relationships that's missing:

_____

_____

How I want to feel in life:

_____

_____

What I want in my life that I don't have:

_____

_____

Negative things in my life that I want removed:

_____

_____

Things I still want to achieve in my life:

_____

_____

What I really want for myself:

_____

_____

How I want to present myself to the world:

_____

_____

Things that would make me feel more confident, capable, and secure:

_____

_____

On pages 37 to 38, you answered several questions. Whether you realize it or not, *this* is your motivation—a description of your *best self!* This is what you will achieve if you conquer your self-sabotage! So take a moment now to rewrite your list of answers into a paragraph. Write it as a series of outcomes you are sure of.

Example: I will have a stable relationship that is intimate and safe, where I feel comfortable being vulnerable. I will feel stable in my life and confident in my decisions without always second-guessing myself. I will feel proud of myself and present that to the world. I will be happy and feel safe and secure.

_____

_____

_____

_____

_____

_____

SECTION 2

Why We Do It

Chapter 7

COGNITIVE DISTORTIONS

"It takes but a handful of words to ambush my soul with hope. Yet, the vexing question in it all is why do I so often ambush the words?"

—Craig D. Lounsbrough

Long before people binge-watched Netflix while staring deadlines in the face or ruined themselves financially with impulse purchases, people were sabotaging themselves—it's not a new phenomenon. There are references to and research about different forms of it that date back centuries. And as long as it has been around, there have been different theories to explain it. For instance:

➡ In 1916, psychoanalyst Sigmund Freud described recurrent experiences with individuals "wrecked by success," tying self-sabotage into the Oedipal Complex of childhood and addressing the fear of success phenomenon.

➡ In 1939, psychoanalyst René Laforgue coined the term "failure neurosis" to address the complex relationship between our desires and our guilt and addressing the fear-of-failure phenomenon.

➡ In 1943, psychoanalyst W. R. D. Fairbairn presented the concept of the "internal saboteur" as an ingrained self-deprecatory part of ourselves, often a representation of an abusive parent.

➡ In 1950, a psychoanalyst by the name of Sándor Lorand coined the term "success neurosis" to describe how people respond to their own success by feeling guilt or attacking themselves in some way.

➡ In 1971, famed psychologist Abraham Maslow used the phrase "Jonah Complex" to describe individuals who were unable to pursue their own goals out of fear (named for the biblical Jonah who attempted to avoid the mission given to him by God).

➡ In 1972, Matina Horner, a psychologist, coined the now well-known term "fear of success" based on anxieties she was seeing college students experiencing in regard to their academic success.

So, as you can see, there have been theories on self-sabotage for as long as there have been theories! Each of them has a different viewpoint of and explanation for the problem, as you can see above. I am going to touch on the most prevalent theories of today: cognitive behavioral psychology, approach-avoidance conflict, and learning theory.

Let's start by looking at cognitive behavioral psychology and the theory of cognitive distortions.

Self-sabotage is rooted in our thinking. If you look back through all the different types of self-sabotage, they are all about the ways we think, the ways we integrate information, and the ways we process sensory information.

Because self-sabotage is rooted in our thinking and causes us to stand in our own way, it *almost always* involves distortions of the truth—a concept called *cognitive distortions*.

Let's look at the concept more closely and discuss how these thoughts create self-sabotage.

Psychiatrist Aaron Beck, noted as the father of cognitive-behavioral psychology, developed the concept of cognitive distortions, which are ways our minds convince us of something that's not really true, rational, or in keeping with logical thinking, and which usually reinforce our negative thinking or emotions. In other words, cognitive distortions are ways we distort the facts or the data to believe something different. That something often forms the root of our self-sabotage. Because many of our actions and decisions are based on these cognitive distortions, they have a lot of influence over how we live our lives.

Here is Beck's list of common cognitive distortions:

1. All-or-Nothing Thinking

2. Overgeneralizing

3. Discounting the Positive

4. Dwelling on the Negative

5. Shoulds, Oughts, and Musts

6. Fortune Telling

7. Mind Reading

8. Personalizing

9. Catastrophizing

Let me give you some examples of how cognitive distortions might play out in relation to self-sabotage. The following are examples of all-or-nothing thinking.

➡ Sheila was on a diet when she went to a Thursday night party. Planning to avoid dessert altogether, Sheila instead found herself polishing off three cupcakes. As a result, Sheila told herself, "I might as well have three more." And since she overindulged on Thursday, she decided to just keep up that behavior all weekend and start her diet again on Monday.

➡ Patty signs up for an online certification program to move up in her career and plans to study for an hour every day for a month. Two weeks into her study plan, Patty accidentally arranges to see a friend at a time that overlaps with her planned study time. Unable to find another time, Patty just skips studying for that day. The next day, she decides she's a failure who can't to stick to her plans and never picks up her books again.

➡ Claire goes out one night and is feeling good about herself. As she stands by the food table snacking, she talks to Sean, a man whom she might be interested in dating. The conversation goes well, and at some point, Claire excuses herself to go to the restroom. She looks in the mirror and notices she has a giant piece of spinach in her teeth. Mortified, she starts thinking about her conversation with Sean and wondering if he was disgusted. He looked away at one point during the conversation and she realizes he must have been trying to find an excuse to get away from her. She is devastated and leaves the party immediately. She lets Sean's call go to voicemail the next day and doesn't get in touch with him again.

Do you recognize this type of thinking? Do any of these thoughts sound familiar to you? Can you relate to having your emotional state dramatically shift based on your own assumptions?

These thoughts are very common cognitive distortions because they don't reflect a rational perspective of reality. They are also clearly forms of self-sabotage. Let's examine the thoughts in these situations in some depth so you can understand how off the mark they really are.

In the first scenario, Sheila ate off-limits foods and felt guilty and discouraged. She decided to stay off her diet until she could get a "fresh start" on Monday. A classic sign of The Overindulger.

So why is this irrational? Well, doing a quick calculation, we can estimate that Sheila ate about 1,500 calories more than she had planned. Realistically, that's not a whole lot to undo.

But Sheila goes through the whole weekend with the "I've blown it. I'll start again on Monday" mentality. That last-chance eating—getting in all of the food that isn't on her diet before she embraces the restrictions again—might drive her to eat an extra 10,000 to 12,000 calories.

Now, *that* is a lot more overindulgent eating to contend with and can lead to more guilt and more discouragement. On top of those feelings, she has to exert much more effort to get back to healthy eating. It's a cycle that feeds on itself and keeps you stuck in place. The constant off-and-on nature of the diet can also lead to other cognitive distortions, which lead to other forms of self-sabotage.

A more logical and rational approach would have been, "I didn't plan for that, but I can return to healthy eating at the next opportunity. There's no reason to wait until after the weekend." She might not have a great result at her next weigh-in, but 1,500 calories extra wouldn't make a massive difference in such a long journey.

In the second situation, Patty broke her plan to study every day of the month by choosing to hang out with a friend. In classic Perfectionist style, she decided that missing that one study day made all her efforts a complete waste of time, so she didn't see any point in continuing. In reality, missing one study session out of the thirty she had planned would not have had a huge effect on her certification process. She wouldn't completely forget everything she already learned in the matter of a day.

She might even have found a real study benefit from simply taking a break to see a friend. She could unwind and get enough energy to study even harder the next day. But by seeing things in all-or-nothing terms—either "I'm sticking to my plan 100 percent" or "I've blown it"—there was no in-between that would have let Patty both prioritize her studying and see a friend when she was available.

In the third situation, Claire started out the evening feeling great about herself. However, Claire is a classic Self-Critic and an Assumer, and she let these tendencies win out. She selectively ignored all the positive evidence that Sean was interested in her despite having food in her teeth, something that happens to almost everyone and doesn't impact who she is as a person. Instead, she focused on the neutral evidence (that she noticed him looking around) and dismissed everything else.

She even continued this belief when he called her—a clear piece of evidence that he was still interested—and yet she continued to ignore that possibility. All of her focus was on that tiny piece of spinach. That type of thinking is not logical, because it doesn't take all the data into consideration. Clearly the data suggested that Sean was interested in Claire, but her self-criticism and her tendency to assume the worst prevented her from seeing that.

Claire's interpretation of the interaction reflects another cognitive distortion called "mind reading." She decided that she "knew" what Sean was thinking despite the fact that there was very limited evidence to support that thought and clear evidence to the contrary.

Looking at all three of these scenarios, it becomes clear that when you don't question automatic thoughts and allow them to influence your feelings and actions, you are at risk of acting on distorted information. To prevent this you need to learn to identify and challenge irrational, and often destructive, automatic thoughts.

It's easier to identify your irrational thoughts and connect them with your personal style of self-sabotage when you become familiar with the different types of cognitive distortions. As we go through them, take note of which ones resonate with you. Your automatic thoughts likely include examples of all the following, but there are probably three or four types of cognitive distortions that really stand out for you.

1. ALL-OR-NOTHING THINKING

What Is It?

Looking at experiences in absolutes or black and white terms. There are no gray areas.

Examples

➡ I can't do everything possible to impress my boss so there's no point in doing anything.

➡ If I can't make it to the gym every day, there's no point in going at all.

➡ I have to be perfect at whatever I do, or I'm a failure.

How It's Distorted

All-or-nothing thinking doesn't account for the value of doing things in moderation. Going to the gym 8 out of 10 days or doing things to impress your boss 80% of the time has immense value. To put it even more simply, something is better than nothing. All-or-nothing thinking discounts the value of taking a moderate, sustainable approach to life, behavior, and social interactions.

How It Causes Self-Sabotage

All-or-nothing thinking sets up self-sabotage by creating excuses to not try. It lets you get out of doing whatever you need to do to achieve your goals, simply because you can't do *everything* to achieve them. If you believe you have to do everything in order to accomplish your goal, you set yourself up to do nothing. As much as we'd like to, no one can do everything at once. By not recognizing and stopping all-or-nothing thinking, you create a cycle of underachievement.

The belief that if you can't do everything you might as well do nothing sets you up to often choose to do nothing. This cognitive distortion is commonly used by The Overindulger and The Perfectionist.

2. OVERGENERALIZING

What Is It?

Viewing a negative event as a pattern of negative events instead of an isolated incident. It often includes words such as *always* or *never*.

Examples

➡ I always blow it in relationships so they never last.

➡ I can't stick with anything.

➡ I never stick to my workout plan.

How It's Distorted

It discounts all the times you do things right, which devalues the positive steps you have taken and overemphasizes the times when you have fallen short.

How It Causes Self-Sabotage

Overgeneralizing sets you up to believe things that simply are not true. By taking an isolated incident and blowing it up into an *always* or a *never*, you start to behave as if this assumption were true. Your mind turns isolated incidents into negative trends, and this misperception convinces you to not try at all, even if you have evidence to the contrary. This cognitive distortion is commonly used by The Avoider and The Self-Protector.

3. DISCOUNTING THE POSITIVE

What Is It?

Dismissing compliments or good experiences as being flukes or exceptions.

Examples

➡ I did well this time, but only because I had help.

➡ Yeah, I had a good week, but that almost never happens.

➡ He only asked me out because he feels sorry for me.

How It's Distorted

It denies you the opportunity to feel good about an event or something you've done. It's similar to overgeneralization; you take positive moments and sweep them all into the "flukes" category instead of seeing them as a possible upward trend. It also diminishes the power of positive events to boost your confidence and create momentum—after all, it was just a "fluke" and doesn't really count.

How It Causes Self-Sabotage

Discounting the positive is an effective way to keep you rooted in self-doubt and keep your self-esteem low. By continually dismissing positive outcomes or feedback, it becomes easier and easier to look at yourself negatively. This makes you lose drive, motivation, and the belief that you deserve anything positive. This cognitive distortion is commonly used by The Self-Critic and The Overthinker.

4. DWELLING ON THE NEGATIVE

What Is It?

Putting extreme emphasis on the negative while discounting any coexisting positives.

Examples

➡ Yeah, I had a good time hanging out with my friends the other night, but no one has called me or reached out to me since then, so they must not like me.

➡ Sure, I stuck with my healthy eating plan. But why does that matter, I'm still overweight!

➡ What difference does it make that I'm learning new skills in this program? I'm still not where I need to be.

How It's Distorted

This thinking makes the negatives significantly more powerful and meaningful than the evidence suggests. It can warp even objectively good evidence into something that *must* be negative or that's bound to become negative over time.

How It Causes Self-Sabotage

Dwelling on the negative is one of the most common cognitive distortions for self-sabotage. By hyperfocusing on the negative, you create a false belief that the cards are always stacked against you. In turn, you lose motivation and the will to pursue your goals—if you think you'll always lose, why would you even start? This cognitive distortion is commonly used by The Self-Critic and The Assumer.

5. SHOULDS, OUGHTS, AND MUSTS
What Is It?

Thinking in terms of "shoulds" without questioning how, when, why, or by whom it has been decided that you "should" do A, B, or C.

Examples

➡ I should never struggle with healthy eating decisions.

➡ I should work out every day.

➡ I should work overtime every day and do a ton of extra work before I ask for that promotion.

How It's Distorted

It's an arbitrary determination based on an extreme idea. This thinking sets you up for failure by establishing unrealistic expectations, ones that even the most disciplined people likely can't uphold 100% of the time. It can deprive you of meaningful experiences by creating arbitrary barriers, like telling yourself that you must reach your body-weight goal before getting back on dating websites.

How It Causes Self-Sabotage

Shoulds, oughts, and musts are rooted in a false belief of how one should behave or what is necessary or appropriate. These beliefs are so firmly held that not following them creates immense guilt and sets us up to believe we are wrong, incapable, and even unworthy. By not achieving their "should," someone might convince themselves that they're a failure and that there's no point in trying. This cognitive distortion is commonly used by The Control Freak, The Perfectionist, and The Overindulger.

6. FORTUNE TELLING
What Is It?

Deciding the outcome ahead of time without knowing for certain. Also known as "predicting the future" or assuming.

Examples

➡ I already know I'm not going to have a good time if I go to that party, so there's really no point in going.

➡ I'm never going to find the man of my dreams, so there's no point in dating or putting myself out there.

➡ I'm only going to be able to get this done with the extra pressure of doing it at the last minute.

How It's Distorted

Even with all the information you could probably gather about a situation, you can't know exactly how something will happen. The future is always an unknown with no guarantees. But by fortune telling, you don't even acknowledge the possibility of a positive outcome and instead live your life based on "knowing" that your future will be a negative one.

How It Causes Self-Sabotage

Fortune telling or assuming is an effective cognitive distortion that makes you believe you know the outcome without giving yourself the chance to actually learn that outcome. By acting on the assumption, you believe you are protecting yourself from risk or danger that may not even exist. Doing so reinforces the behavior (since there's nothing to counter the belief) and allows it to continue. This cognitive distortion is commonly used by The Avoider, The Procrastinator, The Assumer, The Control Freak, and The Self-Protector.

7. MIND READING

What Is It?

Mind reading is deciding you know what another person is thinking, even though they haven't told you themself. Most often, mind reading results in a negative assumption.

Examples

➡ I know he didn't smile at me because he thinks I'm ugly.

➡ My boss hasn't mentioned a promotion at all in the last few months. She must think I'm lazy and unqualified.

➡ I can tell he doesn't respect me because of my weight. He assumes I'm lazy and have no control around food.

How It's Distorted

It's not possible to know with 100% certainty what people are thinking without them telling you. Even if you're good at reading faces, you don't know whether the person's possibly negative feeling is about *you*. If you constantly feel bad about yourself or put yourself down, it's easy to assume that others have negative feelings about you, too. But that's an assumption, which might well be a distorted version of reality.

How It Causes Self-Sabotage

Mind reading is another cognitive distortion based on assuming: these assumptions are about other people's thoughts and beliefs. With mind reading, the assumption is always that another person's thoughts toward you are both negative and true. The mind reader internalizes these projected thoughts, allowing them to slowly chip away at their own self-esteem. As their self-esteem gets lower and lower, they lose the belief in themselves that motivates them to push toward their goals. This cognitive distortion is commonly used by The Self-Critic and The Assumer.

8. PERSONALIZING

What Is It?

Personalizing is taking the behavior of others and making it about you. It is similar to the distortion of mind reading, but it's about the other people's actual behaviors instead of their thoughts. You see yourself as being involved in or the cause of external events without any evidence and without thinking of alternative reasons behind what others do.

Examples

➡ Those girls over there are obviously whispering about me.

➡ They scheduled other people at work to review this data. It must be because I presented the information incorrectly.

➡ My boyfriend canceled our plans for dinner tonight saying he was too busy with work. I know he is really just upset with me for how I acted yesterday.

How It's Distorted

Just like with mind reading, this distortion makes assumptions without looking at any evidence or exploring alternatives. Again, you can't "know" that you are the subject of or the cause of another's behavior without them telling you so. This distortion is rooted in self-absorption.

How It Causes Self-Sabotage

Personalizing creates a self-reinforcing belief that you're causing problems or that others feel negatively toward you. The more these beliefs continue, the more they perpetuate themselves and again, leave your self-esteem significantly impacted. By believing you are always the problem, you are less likely to want to be a part of things, since you think you'll potentially make things worse. This cognitive distortion is commonly used by The Self-Critic and The Avoider.

9. CATASTROPHIZING

What Is It?

Catastrophizing is a way of thinking that takes otherwise benign information and makes it significantly more of an issue. It is the equivalent of making a mountain out of a molehill.

Examples

➡ Since my boyfriend and I had a fight, I'm certain he is going to break up with me.

➡ I didn't meet my deadline at work, so I'm sure I'm going to get fired in the next week or so.

➡ This is way too much work. I don't even know where to start. I'll never get it all done.

How It's Distorted

Catastrophizing assumes that outcomes won't just be negative—they'll be catastrophic. The reality is that the outcomes are usually much more muted or benign, but this belief ignores the evidence and assumes the absolute worst.

How It Causes Self-Sabotage

Catastrophizing assumes the worst outcome. Because the worst outcomes are scary or are things that we want to avoid, we behave in such a way that we don't have to experience those outcomes. This behavior can be the direct form of self-sabotage. We can also use our worst assumptions to decide that our efforts are not worth it, or we might change our behavior to fit with our worst-case assumption. This cognitive distortion is commonly used by The Procrastinator and The Avoider.

SUMMARY

Did you recognize your own thinking in that list of cognitive distortions and see how they connect with the types of self-sabotage discussed in the earlier chapters? Are there some distortions that you can relate to more than others? It's common to have a few "favorites." For example, some of my clients spend most of their days trapped in all-or-nothing thinking (and not just about food and weight). Other clients are so discouraged about their life journey that they consistently predict they will fail. That's a whole lot of fortune telling going on.

There's also a lot more going on with self-sabotage and its origins. It's not *just* based in our thoughts. One of its other roots might surprise you. We'll look into that in the next chapter

> We all do all of the cognitive distortions discussed above. But you definitely lean toward some more than others. Use the worksheet on page 53 to pinpoint your most frequently used cognitive distortions and identify how you use them.

✔ How I Use Cognitive Distortions

Cognitive Distortion	Do I Do It?	If Yes, How?
All-or-Nothing Thinking Looking at experiences in absolutes or black and white terms with no shades of gray.	❑ Y ❑ N	
Overgeneralizing Viewing a negative event as a pattern instead of an isolated incident. Using words like *always* or *never*.	❑ Y ❑ N	
Discounting the Positive Dismissing compliments or good experiences as being flukes or exceptions.	❑ Y ❑ N	
Dwelling on the Negative Putting extreme emphasis on the negative while discounting any coexisting positives.	❑ Y ❑ N	
Shoulds, Oughts, and Musts Thinking in terms of *shoulds* without questioning why or how it has been decided that you should do A, B, or C.	❑ Y ❑ N	
Fortune Telling Deciding the outcome ahead of time without knowing for certain, AKA "predicting the future" or assuming.	❑ Y ❑ N	
Mind Reading "Knowing" what another person is thinking, even though they haven't told you themself.	❑ Y ❑ N	
Personalizing Interpreting others' behavior as being about you. Seeing yourself as the cause of external events without evidence.	❑ Y ❑ N	
Catastrophizing Taking otherwise benign information and making it significantly more threatening.	❑ Y ❑ N	

Chapter 8

BIOLOGY AND REINFORCEMENT

"I decry the injustice of my wounds, only to look down and see that I am holding a smoking gun in one hand and a fistful of ammunition in the other."

—Craig D. Lounsbrough

As we've discussed in the previous chapters, our thoughts are a significant part of why we self-sabotage and how we maintain self-sabotage. But believe it or not, there is an aspect of self-sabotage that is actually rooted in our biology! You might be thinking, "Wow, even our biology fights against us?" Yes, there is actually a part of self-sabotage that is caused by your brain and your innate drives.

In 1935, a psychologist named Kurt Lewin presented a theory on the approach-avoidance conflict, which proposes that all goals essentially have both positive and negative consequences attached to them. For example, if your goal is to get a promotion at work, the positive consequence may be a salary increase while the negative consequence might be having to work longer hours. The fact that both types of consequence exist with our goals creates some internal ambivalence. We want the good but we don't want the bad, and those two drives can counteract each other. As we'll get into, certain elements factor into whether we approach our goal or avoid it. To make matters worse, as we get closer to reaching our goals, the negative consequences can appear more significant, causing us to move toward the "avoid" behaviors more than the "approach" behaviors.

Now, here's how this ties into our biology: dopamine. Dopamine is a neurotransmitter made by your body that is very tied into our reward system. Dopamine is a "feel-good" hormone that is akin to a bit of a high, which is why it is so involved in behavior reinforcement; we do something and get a rush of dopamine, so we are motivated to do that thing again. And when we take steps to achieve a goal, we definitely get a dose of that feel-good hormone. Here's the problem: when we take steps to avoid negative consequences or threats, we *also* get a dose of that feel-good hormone.

Going back to the approach-avoidance conflict, we get that reinforcement for approaching the good (like working toward your promotion) *and* for avoiding the bad (slacking off because you're worried about the extra hours or responsibilities your promotion would bring). Historically, these "threats" that we were avoiding were tangible, like a bear coming to attack us or someone trying to steal our food. Put into that context, it's easy to see how avoidance behaviors would be beneficial.

But nowadays, the threats aren't necessarily life threatening. Possibly being self-conscious in a meeting or the thought of being uncomfortable in a situation won't kill you, but that doesn't matter to our brains. Just the *idea* of avoiding these potentially bad outcomes—even though they may not be real—can reinforce avoidant or self-sabotaging behavior via dopamine.

If we dig deeper into the approach-avoidance conflict, we learn that there are three primary determinants of how we choose whether to approach or avoid: intensity, magnitude, and distance. In other words, we subconsciously make the decision based on how *intense* the drive is, how *powerful* the goal is, and how *close* it is—or how easy it is to achieve.

Let's apply this to a real-world situation. Jill is trying to lose 10 pounds. The positive consequence is that she'll fit into the outfit she bought for her vacation, but the negative consequence is giving up some of her favorite foods. She goes to a birthday party and is determined not to have cake. But the cake is from her absolute favorite bakery, and she hasn't had it in ages.

In this situation, she would weigh the intensity (how strong the call to cake is vs. how strong the call to lose 10 pounds is), the magnitude (the impact of her eating the cake vs. the impact of her restraining from eating the cake), and the distance (how easy it is to eat the cake vs. how easy it is to lose the weight). What do you think will end up happening in this scenario? Well, if you said she would eat the cake, you're probably right. The intensity level is high, since the cake is delicious and right within reach, the impact is pretty low, as it is only one piece of cake, and the distance is really low, too, since the cake is right there.

But what if you changed some of those factors? What if she had to go out to get that cake? In that scenario, the psychological distance would be greater so she might be more likely to pass on it. Or what if the cake were not from her favorite bakery? It wouldn't be as appealing, so she likely wouldn't eat it. We could also change the magnitude by telling Jill how many calories are in the slice of cake. Then she might feel that the number of calories outweighs its deliciousness and again, might be less likely to indulge.

You can clearly see how all of these factors tie into the decision to approach or avoid. But how do you determine how impactful something is going to be, or how significant a decision is, or how close or far the consequence is? What factors play into this quick decision making? To find that out, we need to turn to *reinforcement theory*.

Reinforcement theory is based on the Law of Effect, which essentially says that behavior is determined by its consequences. So we are likely to repeat behavior that has positive consequences and unlikely to repeat behavior that has negative consequences.

It's impossible to talk about reinforcement theory without talking about conditioning. You might be familiar with the concept of conditioning through the famous experiment by Ivan Pavlov, often referred to as "Pavlov's dogs." This experiment demonstrates the concept of classical conditioning, which is simply the idea that with repeated pairings, we tend in our minds to connect two unrelated external stimuli. In the classic experiment, the dogs would salivate when exposed to their bowl of food. But with repeated exposure to pairing the sound of a bell with the presentation of food, the dogs would start salivating simply from the sound of a bell.

Classical conditioning is well known thanks to Pavlov's dogs, but there is another type of conditioning that people are less aware of: operant conditioning. This form of conditioning is a behavior change as a result of reinforcement or punishment—essentially a positive (reinforcement) or negative (punishment) consequence of a behavior makes it more or less likely to occur, respectively.

For instance, if you sing and dance as a child and your parents give you lots of praise and encouragement (reinforcement), you are likely to want to continue that behavior. But if, instead, your parents criticize or ignore your singing and dancing (punishment), you are less likely to continue that behavior.

So how is operant conditioning tied to the approach-avoidance conflict and, by extension, self-sabotage? The connection is that avoidance behaviors and many other self-sabotaging behaviors are majorly reinforced because they remove *the idea* of a negative outcome. I specifically say the *idea* because there doesn't ever have to *be* a negative outcome—just the perceived potential for one.

For example, if you believe going to a party is going to be a miserable experience and you decide not to go, you have removed the idea of that negative outcome by skipping the possibility. *And* you've reinforced the drive to not go to parties. You might even reinforce that idea further with a dopamine boost from the thing you choose to do instead, on top of avoiding the negative outcome you think is real. And yet, you never had any evidence that the party would be terrible—you never needed it. You just needed to *think* it could happen. And voila—operant conditioning.

This experience just needs to happen once to reinforce itself. And when it happens over and over again, you create a strong association that's incredibly difficult to change without resolutely focusing on doing so. Let's look back at all the self-sabotage profiles and see how approach-avoidance conflict and operant conditioning create and reinforce these behaviors.

THE PROCRASTINATOR

The Procrastinator may start by avoiding a task that feels daunting or overwhelming by assuming the avoidance is more beneficial than starting to chip away at the task (*approach-avoidance conflict*). Eventually they take on the task and they do really well. They believe that the procrastination is why they did well—the classic "I work best under a time crunch" thought. And as they continue to operate under this belief, they reinforce this idea and become a habitual procrastinator (*operant conditioning*).

THE OVERTHINKER

The Overthinker generally starts with worry—worry about what's going to happen, what someone is going to do, or how someone is going to respond to them. This worry makes them put off engaging with the thing that's worrying them, a type of avoidance (*approach-avoidance conflict*). And then, the situation they worried about becomes a self-fulfilling prophecy. The Overthinker believes they need to analyze every situation and everyone's behavior because they already think they know the outcome is going to be negative (*operant conditioning*).

THE ASSUMER

The Assumer looks at an upcoming situation and determines what is going to happen before it actually happens. As a result of their assumptions, which might not be based in facts, they decide what they are going to do. Because The Assumer often believes that outcomes are going to be negative, they usually choose to avoid those perceived negative situations (*approach-avoidance conflict*). By avoiding a situation that they think is going to be negative, they reinforce their behavior by removing *the idea* of a negative situation; they never get evidence to the contrary (*operant conditioning*).

THE AVOIDER

The Avoider is the textbook example of combining approach-avoidance conflict and operant conditioning. The Avoider simply avoids most situations that they fear or believe to be anxiety-provoking (*approach-avoidance conflict*). Just like The Assumer, they reinforce their avoidance by *not* having a negative experience and believing that their decision to avoid is what prevented a negative outcome (*operant conditioning*).

THE SELF-PROTECTOR

The Self-Protector believes that there is danger or an attack lying around every corner, and all it takes is *one* situation where attack *was* lying around the corner for them to develop this belief. Because they believe an attack is waiting, they avoid certain situations (*approach-avoidance conflict*). And by avoiding the perceived threat and *not* getting hurt, they again reinforce the idea that staying away from certain situations is keeping them safe (*operant conditioning*).

THE CONTROL FREAK

Like The Self-Protector, The Control Freak avoids situations where they are not in control, giving them the perception of safety. They also over-prepare for situations that they don't or can't avoid, making sure to always have control (*approach-avoidance conflict*). By trying to control everything in a situation or avoiding it altogether, The Control Freak is safe and feels these behaviors are the reasons why (*operant conditioning*).

THE OVERINDULGER

The Overindulger is in a constant battle between approach and avoidance. Most of their behavior is based on avoiding—like a dieter who restricts certain foods that are counter to their goals. When they go into over-indulgence mode, they are all *approach*—such as the dieter who rebels and eats everything in sight (*approach-avoidance conflict*). The back-and-forth nature of The Overindulger makes them believe that they are powerless and have no self-control (*operant conditioning*).

THE SELF-CRITIC

The Self-Critic's approach and avoidance behaviors are based on their self-perception and the beliefs and behaviors that are tied closely to it. The Self-Critic tends to engage in "approach" behaviors when the situation allows them to judge themselves harshly, and avoid situations (or even comments) that might paint them positively (*approach-avoidance conflict*). As a result of emphasizing the negative and ignoring or avoiding the positive, The Self-Critic reinforces their negative beliefs about themselves (*operant conditioning*).

THE PERFECTIONIST

The Perfectionist has incredibly high ideals, and this attitude makes most tasks and opportunities daunting. Without the right conditions, The Perfectionist can easily be overwhelmed by their ideals and simply not engage in or avoid those tasks or opportunities (*approach-avoidance conflict*). Just like The Self-Critic, The Perfectionist starts to feel incompetent and self-critical as a result of not getting anything done (*operant conditioning*).

Our biology is powerful and important—after all, approach-avoidance conflict and operant conditioning kept our ancestors safe from danger and predators, allowing us to be where we are today. Unfortunately, our brains haven't had the time to evolve to logically process what's considered a threat by today's modern standards. But now that we know the second big piece behind self-sabotage, we can dig even deeper into the concept.

> Do you know how the approach-avoidance conflict and operant conditioning help fuel your own personal self-sabotage? Let's dig in and take a look!

✔ How Biology and Reinforcement Maintain My Self-Sabotage

Let's look at how the approach-avoidance conflict and operant conditioning maintain your own personal self-sabotage.

Approach-Avoidance Conflict = reinforcement for both approaching the good and avoiding the bad.

Operant Conditioning = behavioral change as a result of reinforcement or punishment.

Example: Lisa's self-sabotage is seen every time she loses weight. She has a goal of losing 10 pounds. Every time she loses 6 to 7 pounds, she binges and gains all the weight back. The approach-avoidance conflict reinforces her behaviors by causing her to feel like she's been restricted from all these wonderful foods and to believe that she gets to enjoy them only if she binges. As a result of the restriction and the binge-eating behavior, operant conditioning leaves her believing that she has no self-control.

1. My self-sabotage is:

_____

_____

_____

_____

Approach-avoidance reinforced by:

_____

_____

_____

_____

My operant conditioning:

_____

_____

_____

_____

2. My self-sabotage is:

_____

_____

_____

_____

Approach-avoidance reinforced by:

_____

_____

_____

_____

My operant conditioning:

_____

_____

_____

_____

Chapter 9

OTHER CAUSAL FACTORS

"There is stability in self-destruction, in prolonging sadness as a means of escaping abstractions like happiness. Rock bottom is a surprisingly comfortable place to lay your head. Looking up from the depths of another low often seems a lot safer than wondering when you'll fall again. Falling feels awful. I'd rather fucking fly."

—Kris Kidd

The root of our self-sabotage is based on how we think, how we respond to the approach-avoidance conflict, and how, based on those two things, we learn or connect the dots between our situation and the outcome. These aspects of self-sabotage are extremely significant, as they involve processes that we can't readily control, like the release of dopamine or our deeply rooted beliefs about our realities.

But there are other factors that contribute to self-sabotage, too, and these can be instrumental in making it more or less likely to happen. It's worth taking a look at some of those.

ANXIETY

Anxiety often goes hand in hand with worry. Anxiety is essentially how we respond to stress and is most often the fear about what's coming, what's going to happen, or the unknown. Most people have a little bit of anxiety here or there, but for some, anxiety can be severe enough for an anxiety disorder diagnosis. In fact, anxiety disorders are the most prevalent mental illness in the United States, affecting more than 40 million people (making it even more common than depression). For these people, their anxiety is so debilitating that it interferes with their life, their behavior, their jobs, and their relationships, preventing them from going places, doing things, and living life in all sorts of ways.

Anxiety in and of itself is rather like its own form of self-sabotage. Anxiety-based thinking (in the form of worries and fears) is a primary driver in several of the different types of self-sabotage—such as The Avoider being fearful of fear-inducing situations—and is secondary in several others—such as The Control Freak feeling anxious when they can't control something. This doesn't mean that engaging in self-sabotage necessarily indicates that you have an anxiety disorder, but some level of anxiety can easily instigate and perpetuate self-sabotaging behaviors.

Avoidance is the most common way we respond to anxiety—something known to be part of many self-sabotage styles. The other most common response to anxiety is a heightened level of arousal or awareness—a constant overanalysis of everything that's going on around us. You can easily see how that behavior is tied to several of the self-sabotage profiles, such as that of The Overthinker, who zooms in on every potentially negative detail of a situation. Over time, these responses can actually trigger *more* anxiety, creating a chicken-or-egg relationship between anxiety and self-sabotage: you don't know if you're anxious because you're self-sabotaging or if you're self-sabotaging because you're anxious.

SELF-ESTEEM

Self-esteem is a person's feeling of worth or value—essentially how much the person likes and appreciates themself. For the most part, a healthy level of self-esteem is about having a strong feeling of self-worth and valuing oneself in such a way that you see your importance without inflating it and becoming arrogant. Good self-esteem is highly correlated with achievement, attractiveness, and capability. Low self-esteem, on the other hand, is strongly correlated with self-sabotaging behaviors.

Your level of self-esteem determines whether you feel you are or aren't deserving of things—deserving of success, deserving of love, deserving of happiness. If you believe you're worthy of something and want it, then you are most likely going to make it happen. If you don't believe you deserve these things, you probably won't push toward or accomplish your goals, deepening a feeling of worthlessness. If you believe you're not worthy of love, you are not going to put in effort to establish a relationship. If you believe you're not worthy of your dream job, you won't take the steps to get there. The reality is that low self-esteem actually makes achievement feel uncomfortable (more on that later), because you don't believe it's merited or deserved.

On the other hand, self-sabotage can also *cause* low self-esteem. As with anxiety, there is a chicken-or-egg relationship between self-esteem and self-sabotage. By continuing to engage in self-sabotaging behaviors and not allowing yourself to achieve your goals, you can start to feel bad about yourself and your capabilities. Over time, these feelings become more and more deeply rooted until it becomes unclear which is causing the other.

COMFORT ZONE

As human beings, we just do not like to feel uncomfortable, physically or mentally. We will choose comfort and familiarity over almost anything—even happiness. Yes, you read that right: we often choose comfort over happiness. Whatever we are used to—whether it's neglect, abuse, depression, or anything else—is also what we are comfortable with.

Our human desire for comfort is the reason that we stay in unpleasant scenarios and that we often see people choosing to stay in a situation we deem to be negative. You've probably seen or known couples that just don't get along and have thought to yourself, "Why are they still together?" Well, the answer is: it's comfortable. They may not like each other very much, but it's "known." They *might* be happy being single again or with another person, but they don't know whether that's the case. They don't like the unknown, and neither does anyone else, which is one of the reasons we often choose to stay in our comfort zone.

Our need for comfort can also lock us into dysfunctional patterns. That same person who's with a partner they don't get along with might continue to seek out the same kind of person because that's what they're used to. The idea of being with someone who's kind to them or patches up conflicts without blowing up is scary because they don't know what to expect. The simple need for comfort can end up making us seriously uncomfortable in the long run.

Now, let's think about this idea and how it relates to self-sabotage. Most self-sabotage is related to standing in our own way of achieving what we want, the things that we think will bring us happiness. But those things are also probably experiences we've never had or situations we've never been in—reaching a desired weight, running a marathon, starting our own business, anything! Therefore they are *uncomfortable*. Sure, we may be unhappy in our current situation, but at least we're comfortable.

The drive to stay in our comfort zone provides a lot of motivation to self-sabotage. Imagine a friend of yours who's been single for as long as you can remember. They may talk about dating and wanting to find someone to share their life with and may even actively date on occasion. But being single is what they know and is therefore their comfort zone, making the idea of settling down with someone unfamiliar and scary.

That friend is likely to tell themself that a person who clearly is demonstrably interested in them couldn't possibly *really* like them, or that they're not attractive enough to find someone worthwhile. They're sabotaging themself even though they know what they want.

These three aspects of self-sabotage—anxiety, low self-esteem, and the drive to stay in our comfort zone—are important on their own, but they're also important in the context of the biggest driver of them all—*fear*.

It's time to look at some of these other causal factors and see how they may be creating or strengthening your personal self-sabotage.

✔ How Are These Factors Influencing My Self-Sabotage?

ANXIETY

Do I feel worry or anxiety in certain situations?   ❏ Y   ❏ N

Am I fearful or avoidant of certain situations?   ❏ Y   ❏ N

How these factors are contributing to my self-sabotage:

Example: I worry what people will think of me or fear that I'll say the wrong thing and be judged. So I don't go into group settings often.

_____

_____

_____

_____

SELF-ESTEEM

Do I feel down on myself or beat myself up often?   ❏ Y   ❏ N

Am I lacking confidence in many situations?   ❏ Y   ❏ N

Do I feel undeserving of success, achievement, or happiness?   ❏ Y   ❏ N

How these factors are contributing to my self-sabotage:

Example: I often feel I'm not good enough at work and there's no point in trying to get a promotion because I'll eventually be found out as a fraud.

_____

_____

_____

_____

COMFORT ZONE

Do I avoid new situations for fear of being uncomfortable? ☐ Y ☐ N

Do I choose to stay in my comfort zone often? ☐ Y ☐ N

How these factors are contributing to my self-sabotage:

Example: I always fantasize about starting my own business, but it all seems so overwhelming and unknown. I choose to just stay where I am because it feels safer.

_____

_____

_____

_____

Chapter 10

THE ROOT OF SELF-SABOTAGE

"What is required for many of us, paradoxical though it may sound, is the courage to tolerate happiness without self-sabotage."

—Nathaniel Branden

We now have a good grip on the numerous reasons for, and nuances of, our self-sabotage, from cognitive distortions to low self-worth, but we still haven't hit on the basic root of self-sabotage. And we can sum that up with just one word: *fear*. Yes, fear forms the basis for *all* of our self-sabotage, and that fear can take numerous forms.

We've already talked about how anxiety (the fear of what's ahead or what could potentially be coming) can be debilitating. We've also talked about the drive to keep ourselves comfortable and how moving outside of our comfort zone could create fear. But those fears, and all the other kinds of self-sabotage, can be boiled down to two basics: fear of success and fear of failure.

Most people are not surprised to hear that fear of success is a causative factor for self-sabotage. After all, if you are scared of succeeding, it makes sense that you would stand in your own way and prevent yourself from achieving it! But fear of failure is a little more surprising for people to hear. Let's discuss them both in a little more detail.

Fear of success is a pretty common term that I'm sure you've heard. But the concept doesn't really make sense, does it? If you ask most people what they want in life, their answer will likely be some form of success, whether that's a happy marriage, a satisfying career, or financial security. All of these are some form of success, right? So why would we also be *scared* of that success? If it's something we *want*, it should be enticing and attractive, not scary!

There are actually many reasons we may fear success and, not surprisingly, a lot of them circle back to our self-sabotage styles.

One of the first reasons why people fear success is insecurity. Many struggle with the idea of achieving because they feel they simply don't deserve it, a side effect of their low self-worth. Others struggle with "imposter syndrome," where they find themselves questioning whether they are really capable, or able to live up to expectations—often feeling like they're just pretending until someone finds out that they're a fraud. The commonality across all of these individuals is that, regardless of any success that may likely be coming their way, they end up doubting themselves and their abilities, leading them to question whether they can live up to expectations.

Another contributor to fear of success is what I call the *Now What* Effect. Most people work toward a success-based goal for a very long time, like career milestones or weight-loss goals, and put a lot of faith into the outcome. They believe "*this* is the thing that is going to make me happy" or "*this* is the thing that's going to leave me fulfilled." That line of thinking creates two major worries: 1) "What if I'm not happy and not fulfilled after I reach my goal? Then what?" and 2) "I've achieved my goal. Now, what? What do I do then? What do I focus on? Where do I apply my efforts?"

Most of us just don't want to take the risk that we were wrong about the goal making us happy. Additionally, we'd rather keep at it than have to find something new to focus on. As already pointed out, we humans really hate the unknown—and constantly stopping ourselves from reaching our goals keeps us in the safe bubble of doing what we're already familiar with.

A final significant contributor to fear of success is concern over the outcomes or consequences of that success. As I mentioned above, many look to success as the thing that's going to make them happy, and there's a real fear of that not coming to fruition. But there are other outcomes of success that are unappealing, like increased pressure or stress, less free time, a lot more of the unknown—all things we try to avoid. At least with failure, we stay in the "known" territory and don't have to adapt to the new and the unknown, just as we do if we let "what if?" thinking sabotage our efforts.

Let's look at an example of fear of success in action: James has been working hard his whole life at a desk job with the goal of eventually becoming a VP of the company. As that goal gets closer and closer, James starts to question himself and his ability to perform the job. In his head he turns small mistakes with minimal consequences into massive failures, and he wonders if his boss was being truthful when she said she liked his presentation. James wonders if he's even capable of being a VP at all (insecurity). He also starts to wonder what he will focus on once he achieves the promotion and if it will actually make him happy (the Now What Effect).

The more he thinks about it, the more he starts to focus on what the job will *actually* mean: longer work hours, higher stress, more time away from his family, and unfamiliar situations and interactions at work. James soon finds himself missing deadlines and skipping out on work more often without realizing that his fear of success has caused him to self-sabotage.

But what about fear of failure? How does that play into self-sabotage? I mean, self-sabotage is a way to *cause* failure, right? So why would someone self-sabotage and cause failure if failure is what they fear?

First off, as human beings, we generally like to be in control; that is, we like to have some level of control in regard to what happens to us because it makes us feel safer and more secure. It's why we are rarely comfortable putting our fate in someone else's hands—we can't read their minds, so we can't know what they'll do or what the consequences of their actions will be.

While both failure and self-sabotage create the same outcome, one of them allows us to be in control of our fate and the other doesn't. If we fail a test, we would prefer to say that we knew we were going to fail because we didn't study than to be surprised with an F. See the difference? By self-sabotaging, we may still be failing, but we are "in control" of that fate.

Another contributing factor is ego protection. Our egos are all fairly fragile, even if we don't think they are, and are often not strong enough to handle failure that's the result of our being incapable or not good enough. By taking control through self-sabotage, we not only maintain power over our fate, but we follow our natural instinct to protect our fragile egos from feeling incompetent. Using that same example of failing a test, it's not that we are not smart enough to pass. It's simply that we didn't study, so naturally, we failed. It's not that we are not good enough; it's simply that we didn't try. We protect our ego because the consequences don't reflect on us a person, just our behavior.

A final factor here is the avoidance of shame or embarrassment. This may not seem like much, but shame is very deeply rooted. Shame doesn't just make us feel bad about something we've done (like guilt)—it makes us feel bad about who we are as a person. Such a powerful feeling is difficult to shake, making avoidance of shame a compelling goal. As illustrated in the test example above, we would much rather believe and have others think that we failed because we didn't study than believe and have others think that we really were not capable of passing the test.

Essentially, the fear of failure creates self-sabotage through the belief, conscious or unconscious, that if you don't try (self-sabotage), you can't fail (fear of failure).

Both the fear of failure and the fear of success keep us trapped in cycles that only lead us to failure. How do we break free?

Let's take a few minutes to look deeply at your self-sabotage and really understand how these roots—fear of success and fear of failure—are responsible for keeping you stuck.

✔Fear of Success and Fear of Failure in My Self-Sabotage

Let's examine fear of success and fear of failure and identify their role in your own personal self-sabotage.

FEAR OF SUCCESS

Why might the idea of achieving what I want be scary?

Example: I'm scared that finally getting a promotion and being "the boss" mean being overwhelmed with work and expectations and having it pull me away from my family.

_____

_____

_____

_____

_____

_____

FEAR OF FAILURE

How am I stuck as a result of not wanting to fail or to look bad?

Example: I want to go to grad school but I'm afraid my GRE scores won't be good enough, and I won't get in. I'll have to tell people I didn't get in and face all of that shame. I'd rather not try.

_____

_____

_____

_____

_____

_____

What We Can Do about It

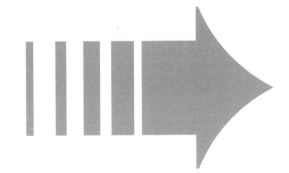

Chapter 11

EXTERNALIZE THE VOICE

*"I wish I could change everything about myself but it's just—it's too late to **do** anything, that's the problem. It's all so fucked up, and I just don't know who I am anymore, you know? Like, who is this person who made all these choices that I just have to live with? I look back at that person and I hate her, I hate her so much for what she did to me, that person is like my nemesis, my worst enemy, but the problem is, that person is me."*

—Kristen Roupenian

Now you know what self-sabotage is, along with how we do it and why we do it. You understand it on all levels and from multiple angles. Now, what? What do you do about it?

The simple answer is *you fight it!* You become a Sabotage Warrior™. And that's exactly what we're going to learn now.

A quick note before we dig in here: Fighting your self-sabotage can't be a passing thing. It's not something you do every now and then, or when you find yourself with a bit of free time. This needs to be a commitment. A commitment to making true, sustainable change. A commitment to focus, to make a continuing effort, and to truly avoid self-sabotaging your attempts to stop self-sabotaging!

This is a process involving the development of skills, meaning that the more you do it, the better you get at it. Since we are becoming Warriors, let's use a boxing example. When someone first starts out boxing, they don't get thrown into the ring with the heavyweight champion of the world. They start out practicing, learning beginner skills like throwing a jab or dodging an opponent's attacks. Then later, when they are ready, they start competing in amateur bouts.

But just because they do well in practice doesn't mean they'll win every time. They'll struggle and lose quite a few fights, especially at first. Slowly, gradually, they get stronger and stronger and more capable. Eventually they even start to win. They become confident in their skills and know that even if they break their winning streak, they can keep working to improve.

That is how a Warrior develops. They build skills, and keep honing them and sharpening them, getting stronger as a result. That is exactly what you are going to do in your process to become a Sabotage Warrior.

I started this book by telling you that you have a voice in your head. As you've been reading through this book, you've probably recognized several things that you have heard that voice say to you *many* times over in your lifetime. I want you to take a moment to really focus on that voice. You are not crazy and I know you don't actually have someone living in your head, but I want you to start thinking and acting as if you do! Think of some of the things that that voice says to you over and over.

Maybe it tells you that you are not good enough. Maybe it tells you certain behaviors are too risky. Maybe it tells you this one time won't matter. Maybe it tells you that you'd be safer *not* doing than doing. Whatever it tells you, I want you to take a moment and really *hear* that voice. In fact, stop looking at this page for a moment and close your eyes and *listen* to that voice talking to you. Really *hear it*–hear the voice talking to you. I'll wait.

Okay, so you've paid some attention to that voice in your head. Now, without thinking too hard about this, I want you to give the voice a name. Whatever name just popped into your head, *that's it!* Don't struggle with it—whatever you just came up with is right. You've just named your sabotage voice.

I want to talk a little bit about what we just did and why we did it. You see, your sabotage voice is standing in your way of achieving success; it's preventing you from living your dreams and reaching your potential. By naming it, it's easier to fight because it's outside of yourself. It's significantly easier to beat something when it's *not* you.

If your sabotage voice were a friend or someone you knew, you would probably think that person was an asshole, right? Well that's *exactly* how I want you to start thinking of your sabotage voice: as an asshole that's out to get you. If someone in your life told you that you were not good enough, or that you shouldn't bother trying, or that you're best off avoiding the things that could bring you joy, what would you say to them? You might call them out, stand up to them, tell them they are wrong, or simply disconnect from them. The problem with your sabotage voice is that it has always been a part of you so you couldn't respond in one of these ways—until now.

Now that you have named your sabotage voice (for the sake of our discussion here, we'll use the name Sabby), you can start to think of it as someone other than yourself, someone who is mean and nasty and out to get you. But thankfully, they're also someone you can ignore, someone you can yell or curse at—someone you can *fight!*

Let's get a little more of an understanding of Sabby. Sabby's entire purpose in life is to stand in your way and to prevent you from achieving your goals. Sabby likes nothing more than to see you fail or not try—it brings them joy. Sabby's favorite thing to do is to pick fights with you and take advantage of you when you are weak. Sabby loves to take joy away from you. Sabby is a mean and nasty person. Every time Sabby wins one of these battles, Sabby gets stronger and you get weaker.

You've probably been battling with Sabby for a long time, and Sabby has probably won—a lot. That makes Sabby super strong, making you super weak. Think of yourself as a beginner boxer who is just learning how to fight. You're gonna go through some drills, develop some skills, and start battling. And eventually, you will start winning. Not all the time, but certainly some of the time. And every time you win, Sabby gets just a little weaker. And the more you fight, the more you win. And the more you win, the weaker Sabby gets. You can take away Sabby's power battle by battle and get your life back. It's how you become a Sabotage Warrior. So let's start fighting.

Now that we know your sabotage voice is external and we even have a name for it, we are going to make sure you have a really clear picture of that sabotage voice on page 80!

✔ My Sabotage Voice

You should have a name for your sabotage voice now. (If not, take a moment to come up with one). Now, I want you to *really* think about this saboteur and get a picture of them in your head. Think about their personality and traits, get a real feel for them, and write it all down!

My sabotage voice is:

_____

What he/she looks like:

Examples: Slicked-back hair, curly mustache, beady eyes. Hunched over, wild hair, wart on nose.

_____

_____

_____

_____

_____

A little more about my sabotage voice:

Example: mean and calculated, angry and bitter, always trying to attack me and prevent me from having any joy or happiness in my life.

_____

_____

_____

_____

_____

Chapter 12

LEARN YOUR OPPONENT'S STYLE

"Stop standing in your own way. Stop making excuses. Stop talking about why you can't. Stop sabotaging yourself. Decide which direction you are going in and take action. One decision at a time, one moment at a time."

—Akiroq Brost

After naming your sabotage voice, you're probably already pulling on your metaphorical boxing gloves to start building up your Sabby-fighting skills, right? Well, a beginner boxer learning how to fight their opponent needs to get familiar with their opponent's style. That's why boxers are always watching video footage of their opponent's fights—they learn how their opponent moves and how their opponent attacks, so they can learn to defeat them.

It is no different for you in your fight with Sabby. You need to get intimately familiar with how Sabby attacks. You may have thought about this a lot in reading the first two sections of this book, but now you are looking at it as the voice of Sabby, not you. Fighting an outsider changes your perspective on their attacks and gives you new insight into their behavior.

For example, maybe Sabby gets louder and attacks more when you've been in a situation that made you insecure, like an awkward interaction at a grocery store. Or maybe Sabby always pipes in when it's late at night and you can't sleep. Or perhaps Sabby tries to take advantage of you when you are PMSing or when you are tired. These are things we need to know to get familiar with our opponent's style.

We may not have videos to review, but we have the next best thing: thinking through our history. Let's start with the very recent past—think about the last twenty-four hours. Did you hear Sabby in the last twenty-four hours? If so, what did they say to you? How powerful or persuasive were they? And what situation were you in at the time? You can write some notes here:

_____

_____

_____

_____

_____

_____

Let's look back even further. How has Sabby chimed in over the past week? Think about what you've done, where you've gone, and whom you've talked to, and spend some time questioning how Sabby may have talked to you during those situations.

Finally, think about situations over the past week in which you've had negative emotions. Situations in which you've felt insecure, sad, nervous, jealous, scared, or anxious, or experienced some other unpleasant emotion. Think through that situation and ask yourself if Sabby was there. Was Sabby contributing? Was Sabby taking advantage of your feeling that way? Or worse yet, was Sabby the *reason* you were feeling that way? Let's explore this through an example: Janice is at a bar waiting for a friend when she spots an attractive guy walking in. He keeps catching her eye all evening, but instead of thinking, "Maybe I should go talk to him," Sabby pops in to say, "He'd never seriously go out with someone like you, especially when there are prettier women in here. Don't even bother."

Janice takes Sabby's hit right on the jaw, feeling unattractive and sad. She is miserable the rest of the evening even though she should be having fun with her friend.

Sabby attacked Janice in a social setting, talking her out of going up to a guy who seemed interested. Sabby's mean voice made her feel like she wasn't pretty, even though the guy was looking at her. If Janice starts to notice that Sabby tends to attack her when a guy seems to pay attention to her, she'll eventually learn how to fight back.

I want to encourage you to spend the next week really looking for and listening for Sabby. I want you to take note of what they say, as well as the situation or environment you are in when they speak up and the way you feel when they talk to you.

What types of things do they say? Do they try to talk you into anything? Talk you out of anything? Shoot you down or take away your confidence?

Use the worksheet below to go through the last week in the way I've just described. Start to identify where and how Sabby contributed, and anything you can recall about what that sabotage voice said.

Let's keep that focus going and listen for Sabby as we move forward. These are things we need to truly understand if we're going to start fighting Sabby—what they look like, when they strike, what they say. Think of yourself this week as being a boxer watching videos of their opponent's fights—you're researching Sabby's style and approach. Knowing what Sabby's jabs and punches look like will set you up to start winning the fight!

Let's track your Sabby on pages 84 to 87 and really learn your opponent's fighting style!

✔Tracking My Sabotage Voice (Last Week)

Time	Location/Context	What Sabby Said

☑Tracking My Sabotage Voice (Last Week)

Time	Location/Context	What Sabby Said

✔Tracking My Sabotage Voice (This Week)

Time	Location/Context	What Sabby Said

☑ Tracking My Sabotage Voice (This Week)

Time	Location/Context	What Sabby Said

Chapter 13

FIGHT WITH LOGIC AND DISENGAGEMENT

I guess what I am trying to say is that if you want something, you have to take action. A little step toward it every day. Then there is a reason to feel accomplished every day. Match your energy and vibration with what you envision. Believe. You deserve success, so go for it."

—Riitta Klint

I hope you've spent the last week tracking your Sabby's voice and really paying attention to what they had to say and how they said it. You should now be much more familiar with your Sabby's fighting style. That's going to give you the upper hand in starting to fight back.

We're going to start by looking at two different styles of responding to Sabby: *Logic* and *Disengagement*. Let's start by looking at how to fight back with logic.

Look back through your Sabby tracker over the last week and notice what Sabby had to say. I'm going to assume that if you dig into it, most of it is not even remotely rooted in logic. In fact, much of it is probably completely illogical!

I don't know exactly what your Sabby has had to say over the past week, so for examples I'm going to address some common Sabby attacks I hear from my patients:

➡ You always fail, so there is no point in trying.

➡ It's not going to be a good (or fun, enjoyable, or happy) experience, so don't bother.

➡ Unless it's perfect, it's not worth it.

➡ You are just going to end up getting hurt, so you need to protect yourself.

➡ You already screwed up—might as well screw up more!

You can probably take any one of these examples and customize it to fit your particular Sabby. Perhaps your Sabby attacks you about your weight. In that case, they may tell you that you always fail at diets, so there is no point in trying to lose weight. Or maybe they say you can't follow the diet perfectly, so it's not worth trying. Or that you've blown your diet with that cupcake, so you might as well just eat everything in sight.

Perhaps your Sabby holds you back career-wise. If this is the case, they may tell you that you didn't get the promotion last time, so you shouldn't waste time trying for it again. Or they may remind you how awful it felt to not get the promotion and how you shouldn't put yourself through that for a second time. Or maybe they just tell you you're not good enough for the promotion and you don't deserve it.

Maybe your Sabby is always focused on holding you back in your social life. In that case, they may tell you you've been hurt in relationships in the past, so it's not worth trying to find someone new. Or maybe they tell you that you aren't going to succeed in making friends, so it's not worth going to events where you might meet people. Or Sabby might say that you've lost friends in the past and will continue to lose them.

And do you know what all of these Sabby attacks have in common? They are all completely *illogical*— every single one. None of them are rooted in logic, facts, or rational thinking. They just attack you emotionally.

Sabby doesn't have to use logic in their fights because they're trying to hit you on your emotions, not your rational perspective. If Sabby hit you in your logic center every time, they'd lose. So Sabby says things that actually don't make a lot of sense because they know you'll just allow them to hit you emotionally without thinking about how they got that punch in.

But what if you started to look at Sabby's words from a logical framework?

Let's take the following example: "You always fail, so there is no point in trying." Is that a logical statement? Do you *always* fail? Have you failed at every single thing you've ever done in your life?

Of course not! You don't always fail. Like everyone else on the planet, you sometimes fail. But that doesn't mean you should never try, or that success isn't out there for you. It is completely *illogical* to think you should never try because you have occasionally failed.

If you look at anyone you know who is in a successful relationship, they are in that relationship because every single one of their previous relationships ultimately failed.

If you look at anyone who has lost weight and successfully kept it off, they probably have stories of their dozens of previous, unsuccessful attempts at weight loss before they found a diet that worked. If you ask anyone who's ever gotten a promotion, they can also tell you about all the times someone else got the promotion instead.

What that essentially means is that you fail every time, until you don't. So, through this lens, failure is not an endpoint unless you decide to stop trying.

USING LOGIC TO OVERCOME ILLOGIC

Let's go back to the example of Sabby saying, "You always fail, so there is no point in trying." If we look at this as the illogical statement it is, then we can fight back with logic. And by fight back, I mean respond to Sabby. Address precisely what they're saying, but with logic instead of emotion. Here are some examples:

➡ "That is not true—I have succeeded plenty of times in my life!"

➡ "There is always a point in trying; it only takes one time to get it right, and if I don't try, that won't happen!"

➡ "Everyone has failures. It's how we learn and move forward. Every new attempt is a chance to get it right!"

➡ "I'm growing and changing, and giving in means giving up on my dreams; I'm not going to do that!"

Do you see what I mean here by fighting back with logic? These are all powerful statements that effectively leave Sabby powerless. They were trying to hurt you through your emotions, but you blocked that punch and hit Sabby with an unexpected left hook. They were totally unprepared for that, like a fighter going into the ring against someone they've never seen before, so they have no way to respond. *That's* how you win the fight!

I want you to revisit your Sabby tracker from last week and look at how you can respond to Sabby's words with logic instead of emotion. Can you find where they've been illogical? If so, how can you respond with logic? Use the worksheet on page 94 to identify some logical responses (your surprise left hooks) that you can prepare yourself with so you have a brand-new way to respond that leaves Sabby speechless the next time they attack. *Point to you!*

USING DISENGAGEMENT TO DISEMPOWER THE SABOTEUR

You also have another option besides logic: disengagement. I often say to my patients that you can't fight if only one person is fighting, and that is equally true of a fight between you and your Sabby. Sabby wants you to engage. They're itching to get under your skin, to get a rise out of you, to make you feel a certain way and behave accordingly. But what if you don't engage? What if you never get into the ring with them? What if Sabby is throwing punches, and they just bounce right off of you? You essentially take away their power.

If you are going to respond to Sabby with disengagement, it can be really helpful to have a few short and sweet statements prepared to use whenever you hear Sabby start to attack. These are statements that shut Sabby down and remove you from the fight—essentially making it so there is no fight.

Imagine a situation where someone comes up to you and says, "Hey, I don't like you. Let's go outside and fight." What would you do in that situation? You might simply walk away. Maybe you say, "No, thank you." Perhaps you say, "I'm sorry to hear that, but I'm not interested in fighting." I'm guessing for most of you reading this, you don't actually say "Okay!" and then go outside and fight this person.

Think of your Sabby as a person asking you to go outside and fight. Disengagement is the way you remove yourself from that situation. Of course, you can just say, "No, thank you," but with Sabby, the stronger and more powerful the response is, the more likely you are to get them to leave you alone.

Let's again use the example of Sabby saying, "You always fail, so there is no point in trying," but instead of fighting back with logic, you are choosing to disengage. Here are some ways you could respond that achieve that:

➡ "Nice try, Sabby—I'm not going to fight you."

➡ "You are a bully, and I'm not going to let you bully me!"

➡ "I refuse to listen to you!"

➡ "You are mean and cruel, and you don't have power over me!"

➡ "Oh, shut up and leave me alone." (Said loftily, as to an importunate nag.)

Can you see how these statements could end the fight? They are simple and direct, and you can use them in just about any situation when Sabby chimes in. (Of course, you are welcome to use stronger language in your actual response!)

What is your go-to disengagement response going to be when Sabby starts a fight and you don't want to engage? I would encourage you to come up with a few of them. Test them out and find the one that feels the most powerful.

Use the worksheets from this chapter as your homework for this week. You now know how to fight Sabby with logic and some disengagement statements. And I want you to practice using both. When you find Sabby speaking up, practice these strategies and take note of what worked best in what situation.

And remember, this is practice! You are just starting to learn and apply these skills, so don't expect a 100% success rate. Even if you succeed 25% of the time, that's 25% more than you did before, and that is an amazing step forward! After all, you fail until something works!

Now, it's time to create some logical responses. Use the worksheet on page 94 to take some common Sabby statements and create your own logical responses. Then come up with your go-to disengagement statement for when you just need to shut Sabby down.

☑ Logical Fighting and Disengagement Plan

Sabby Comment	My Logical Fight Back

My Sabby Disengagement Responses:

Example: *"I'm not going to listen to you"; "Shut up and leave me alone!"*

_____

_____

_____

_____

_____

_____

_____

_____

_____

_____

_____

_____

_____

_____

Chapter 14

FIGHTING WITH OPPOSITE ACTION

"It was very humbling to realize that my worries were there just to make me miserable. It was even more humbling to realize that I was the guy who had his finger firmly pressed on the misery button. It was wonderful, though, to discover that I also had the power to quit pressing the button."

– Gay Hendricks

I hope that you've had some success this week in fighting your Sabby through logic and disengagement. But as I mentioned in the previous chapter, this may not be the only way to fight. After all, boxers have several different punches, not just one or two. If you always throw the same punch, your opponent will know exactly what it looks like when you're winding up and how to dodge your strike. That's exactly what Sabby will do if you only use one or two techniques to fight them.

We want to arm you with numerous different punches so your Sabby never knows what to expect.

The next "punch" comes from the world of dialectical behavior therapy (DBT), which is an offshoot of cognitive behavioral therapy (CBT), which we discussed earlier. DBT was developed in the 1980s by therapist Marsha Linehan to treat people with borderline personality disorder. Because those in this population tend to experience extreme negative emotions and to have difficulty with emotion regulation, DBT focuses on providing balance, acceptance skills, and distress tolerance.

One skill that DBT teaches is called opposite action. Opposite action helps you regulate emotions by understanding when emotional responses are unjustified, inappropriate, or extreme. By identifying an emotion (anger, sadness, shame, or anything else), we can then identify what urges come up for us when we're in that state of mind. Then we can choose to respond differently, or, in many cases, do the *opposite* of what our natural urge is telling us to do.

For example, we may identify that we are feeling anger when our partner makes an honest mistake, and that the urge associated with anger is to yell at them. Knowing that, we can instead respond with the opposite action—showing warmth or compassion. We may identify that we're feeling sad, which presses us to withdraw and avoid others. Instead of proceeding with that urge without a second thought, we can respond with an opposite action of engaging with others. If we know we're scared, we might feel compelled to move away from whatever is scaring us. By going with the opposite action, we can move toward it, choosing courage over fear.

Opposite action is meant as a tool for managing unrealistic or overexaggerated emotional responses, but it can be easily tweaked to make it a tool or a "punch" that you use to fight your Sabby. Think about the types of emotions Sabby tends to instill in you: fear, shame, guilt, sadness. These all have an associated urge, like running away or avoiding.

That urge is essentially what Sabby is trying to push us into when they attack. Sabby says things to make you feel fear, so you retreat. Sabby says things to make you feel shame, so you beat yourself up. That urge you feel in response to the emotion is exactly what Sabby wants and, often, exactly what Sabby gets. But what if they *didn't* get that response? What if you responded with the *opposite* of what Sabby wanted? That would definitely be a punch that Sabby wasn't expecting!

Let's imagine some examples. Maybe you are feeling low on yourself—you might have had a bad interaction with someone or might be feeling like you don't have many friends. Sabby takes advantage of that by telling you not to go to a party because no one will like you or want to talk to you. The response Sabby expects (and has often gotten!) is for you to stay home and decide Sabby was correct, further feeding their confidence.

But what if you did the exact opposite? What if you went to the party, talked to lots of people, and made some friends? Then what would Sabby have to say the next time this situation arose? Obviously, they wouldn't be able to say the same old same old, because *now* you have concrete evidence that Sabby was lying to you!

Here's another way I like to think about opposite action: it's the idea of playing an acting game. This is a game where you *act like* a person that Sabby does not want you to be. Maybe you act like a person who's confident, or a person who doesn't run from fear, or a person who does things ahead of time instead of waiting until the last moment. This *acting like* helps you to build up even more evidence to shut Sabby down, since Sabby can't point to instances where you prove their point!

Let's think about some scenarios where opposite action or this acting game may work for you. Again, look through your history of Sabby's comments and identify the types of behaviors Sabby encourages you to display. Now, identify what your opposite actions could be. How could you behave in a way Sabby is completely not expecting? How could you respond to take all the wind out of Sabby's sails? What response might make Sabby unable to approach you the same way ever again?

Here's what this could look like: your Sabby might *love* to tell you that you're not worthy of a romantic relationship, which makes you cancel dates and avoid going out to places where you could meet someone. Sabby wouldn't expect you to get all dressed up and walk into your dates with confidence. Sabby *really* wouldn't know what to do if you went out of your way to talk to that person you find attractive at a bar or to message several people on a dating site. Sabby's attacks would bounce right off of you.

Make a point of identifying the opposite actions that you want to try, and post this worksheet somewhere visible: on your fridge, bathroom mirror, phone home screen—wherever you need it to be so you don't forget about it!

You could even consider recruiting a friend. For example, if Sabby often talks you into saying "no" to social events and your opposite action plan is to say "yes" next time, tell your friend to hold you accountable for going no matter what. Now, the next time Sabby speaks up, you are ready to go with your opposite action!

> Use the worksheet on page 100 to create some opposite action
> plans that you can use the next time Sabby tries to attack.

☑ Using Opposite Action

Sabby Comment	Opposite Action Plan

Chapter 15

FIGHT OUR FEARS WITH SYSTEMATIC DESENSITIZATION

"Sometimes we self-sabotage just when things seem to be going smoothly. Perhaps this is a way to express our fear about whether it is okay for us to have a better life. We are bound to feel anxious as we leave behind old notions of our unworthiness. The challenge is not to be fearless, but to develop strategies of acknowledging our fears and finding out how we can allay them."

—Maureen Brady

Now, we're going to continue adding to our arsenal of punches by taking a look at another therapeutic tool called systematic desensitization (SD). SD was developed in the 1950s by a South African psychiatrist named Joseph Wolpe. SD is a type of behavioral therapy based on the principles of conditioning (something we talked about earlier as a contributor to self-sabotage). SD has primarily been used as a treatment for phobias (fears), with the goal of removing the fear response to the phobia source and replacing it with a calm response through counter-conditioning.

The SD approach has three phases: first, the individual learns a technique for relaxing their muscles, combined with breathing exercises. Second, the individual ranks how much fear their phobia would provoke depending on how they interacted with each fear stimulus, creating what is called a hierarchy of stimuli. It typically goes from least fear-provoking to most. Third, the individual slowly exposes themself to the items on their hierarchy while pairing that exposure with the relaxation and breathing techniques.

Let me give you a real-life example of what this might look like. Jane is deathly afraid of spiders and seeks treatment for this phobia. She first learns a series of muscle relaxation techniques and breathing exercises. Then she develops a hierarchy of her fears. It looks like this:

1. Thinking about spiders

2. Seeing pictures of spiders

3. Seeing a spider through a window

4. Seeing a spider across the room

5. Seeing a spider within a few feet

6. Having a spider crawl on her

Now that she has the hierarchy developed, Jane starts her exposure. Jane starts her muscle relaxation and breathing exercises, and then begins thinking about spiders. She does this repeatedly until the thought of spiders fails to elicit any type of anxiety. Then she moves on to number 2 in the hierarchy until that doesn't incite anxiety, either; then she does the same thing with number 3, and so on.

The goal of this type of treatment is to stop certain fear stimuli from creating anxiety. Because anxiety manifests as tension in the body, the exposure pairs relaxation with situations or images that previously elicited anxiety responses and intends to "condition" them away.

You may find yourself asking, what does this have to do with me? I don't have a fear of spiders! Well, SD is a treatment approach meant to address and diminish fears and, as you may recall, most self-sabotage is rooted in fear. So you actually do have phobias! Technically speaking *achievemephobia* is the fear of success and *atychiphobia* is the fear of failure, so there you go.

Of course, this type of fear is not the same as Jane's fear of spiders, so it can't be addressed in exactly the same manner, but we can certainly use aspects of SD to make some changes and fight our Sabby's attempts to keep us stuck. Let's look at how we can do this.

In Chapter 10, you identified some of your fears related to success and failure. Now, we are going to dig into them a little deeper. Go back to your fear list on page 73 and pick one to spend time on.

Really think about it. Close your eyes and visualize it. When you imagine that success or failure, what is it that is *really* scary about it? What is it that you truly fear?

Maybe you've identified a fear of success and, looking deeper, you find that you're truly afraid of being found out as a fraud, getting laughed at, being embarrassed, or feeling disgraced. Or maybe you fear success because you're overwhelmed by the expectations that go along with that success. You fear having your family be completely reliant on you and the possibility of buckling under that pressure. You fear having important deadlines at work and not being able to meet them. You fear having employees underneath you and not being enough of a role model to them.

Or maybe your fear of failure is so strong that it keeps you from trying. And digging into that fear, it's really rooted in shame—having to tell your parents that you didn't succeed, having your boyfriend or girlfriend look at you with disappointment, feeling judged by those around you.

Now, it's time to really look into those fears. Go back to your identified fear (whether it be success or failure or both) and pick it apart. Ask yourself what factors associated with that fear are *really* scary. What parts of it *really* cause anxiety? What situations or expectations are you *really* trying to avoid? Take some time and write them out on your worksheet.

Once you have your list, let's create your hierarchy, ordering the items from least anxiety-provoking to most anxiety-provoking. Let's use the fear of success example from above. Not being a good role model to the employees beneath you might be the least anxiety-provoking, while having your family be entirely reliant on you might be the most. Once you have your hierarchy, we can start pairing your specific fears with relaxation techniques.

You can find a quick guide by Therapist Aid on YouTube, called "How to Do Progressive Muscle Relaxation." Progressive muscle relaxation is a simple process of just tensing and releasing the muscles throughout your body to release tension and create physical relaxation. Give it a shot—it's only a few minutes—so you can get familiar with the process and be able to do it on your own.

It's worth noting here that your Sabby may have already started chiming in on this ("This is stupid!," "I'm not doing this hippie stuff!," "I don't need this—relaxing my muscles isn't going to change anything!"). If you hear Sabby saying something like that, use the skills you've already developed to shut them down. You can out-logic Sabby by telling them that this is a research-backed technique that has been successfully used for decades, or reminding them that there's never any harm in trying. Or you can simply shut Sabby down by telling them to shut up or back off or leave you alone! The important part is to acknowledge when Sabby is talking, without believing their comments.

Once you are familiar with your process, if your anxiety doesn't go away immediately, I want you to pick number one on your hierarchy (the least anxiety-provoking) and do a quick progressive muscle relaxation exercise and visualize that situation. Imagine all aspects of that feared situation and visualize the outcomes, responses, behaviors, and emotions.

Let's go back to the example of being a bad role model to employees beneath you if you get a certain position. Think about how you might fail to help a junior employee who really needs guidance, or how you might not have the right answers to someone's problems. Imagine every outcome you can think of and how they'd make you feel.

It may cause anxiety, but don't worry about that—just let yourself feel it, and keep breathing. Tomorrow, you can come back to this item and do it again. The goal is to keep at it until thinking about the item no longer creates anxiety. At that point, you move on to the next item on your hierarchy.

Again, if your anxiety doesn't go away immediately, Sabby may chime in early on to tell you this whole thing is pointless. You can again respond with logic by telling Sabby that that's not the way it works—it takes several rounds of visualized exposure to get rid of the anxiety.

This tool to fight Sabby does take time, but it can be incredibly effective. Think of it like adding a little bit of armor to yourself, one piece at a time. By the time you work up to the top of your hierarchy and disassociate anxiety with that fear, you'll hardly feel Sabby's attacks.

Use the worksheet on page 105 to write out your fears and then rank order them. Then use the second grid to rewrite them in order.

✓ Using Systematic Desensitization

My Fears	Rank Them 1 to 10

MY FEAR HIERARCHY	
1.	
2.	
3.	
4.	
5.	
6.	
7.	
8.	
9.	
10.	

Chapter 16

CONFIDENCE BUILDING

"Focus on rewarding and praising yourself instead of degrading and punishing yourself. You'll get far better results!"

—Akiroq Brost

As we identified earlier, a lot of self-sabotage is rooted in poor self-concept or low self-esteem. So a natural way to fight self-sabotage (and advance in numerous different ways!) is to work on building your self-esteem. Obviously, this topic is so expansive that I could devote a whole different book to it, so for our purposes here, I'm just going to touch on a few different confidence-building techniques that will help you fight your Sabby.

1. CREATE YOUR "WHY I'M GREAT" MATRIX

I don't know you, but I know that there are lots of great things about you. I know you have many wonderful qualities, from kindness to intelligence to wit. I know you are skilled in certain areas, whether that's in the arts, the sciences, or anywhere in between. And I know you've had successes and achievements in your life, both big and small. I'm guessing you pay very little attention to those great things. In fact, I bet you pay *way* more attention to the skills you don't have than to the skills you do have. Or, you probably hyperfocus on an attribute you wish you had instead of embracing all the wonderful attributes that you do have. I know this because most of us do the same thing—you're not alone in dwelling on the negative.

The reality is that there is so much that is great about you, but you are ignoring it and focusing on the minority of things that you might not be great at. This exercise is a way to help you focus on the positive and to make it a lot harder to ignore all the things that are truly great about you.

In this exercise you will go through a process of identifying what's great about you and plugging it into the "Why I'm Great" matrix. You will be looking at four areas: your qualities or fixed assets; your skills or abilities; your behaviors or actions; and your successes or achievements.

Let's start with your qualities. These are fixed assets—things that don't change or don't require you to do anything. They are just a part of you. It might be that you really like your eye color or your beautiful skin. Perhaps you really like your voice or your long, graceful fingers. Maybe you enjoy being able to see or hear long distances. Perhaps you were born with perfect pitch, or you've had an impeccable sense of rhythm ever since early childhood. Maybe you often get compliments on your petite nose or your lovely ankles.

The point is to address all the little details. Nothing is off limits. You may see some wrinkles under your eyes and decide you don't like your eyes. But don't hyperfocus on one "flaw"—you might miss out on other great attributes around it. For instance, your eyes might be a beautiful color or maybe the shape of your eyes is exactly what you want them to be. Your eyelashes could be long and full, too. You would miss all of those great things if you just saw the wrinkles. The point of this exercise is to give all of those other qualities some much-needed attention.

Now, let's move on to your skills or abilities. These are things you are good at. This could be work-related talents, interpersonal skills, physical abilities, or talents in any other area where you may stand out in the crowd. Maybe you rock at a certain video game or can do a backbend from all of those years of yoga. You might easily read a long book in three days or have a knack for organizing. Or perhaps you're a great listener or always make people laugh with your jokes. The idea is to scour your brain and your knowledge of yourself to come up with all of your skills and abilities—regardless of what they may be.

Next, we're going to look at your behaviors or actions. These are things you do or behaviors you engage in, like donating your time to help out a charity once a month or taking time out to call your mom because you know she's lonely. Perhaps you're a loyal friend whom everyone can count on when they're struggling. Maybe you're a great peacemaker or often help with conflict resolution at work, managing to stay patient and calm when others would get angry. These are things you *do* that are a part of who you are.

Finally, we are going to look at your successes or accomplishments. While this certainly can be degrees or promotions, those are not the only things that represent achievement. An accomplishment could be helping a friend get a job or helping your mother consolidate her debt. It could be finishing a major task at work or successfully saving up money for something you've wanted for a long time. Learning another language is certainly one, as is following through with a dream of backpacking through Europe. Maybe you endured some trauma and successfully recovered and moved forward. This category can be broad—don't sell yourself short by leaving off times you overcame hardship or achieved goals you set for yourself.

Here's an example matrix to work from:

Qualities	Skills
Nice eye color	Fast runner
Pretty smile	Good public speaker
Full lips	Well organized
Clear Skin	Good event planner
Slim legs	Great computer skills
Clear voice	Good teacher
Good eyesight	Good at video games
Good hearing	Great reader
Good sense of rhythm	Flexible
Behaviors	**Accomplishments**
Friendly to others	Put self through college
Kind	Moved to a new city on my own
Generous	Set my personal best running record this year
Willing to share time and resources	Learned a new computer program
Loyal to my friends	Supporting self for the past five years
Always there for my friends	Maintained a job for the past two years
Good team player	Got acknowledged at work recently
Regular volunteer	Saved up for an apple watch
Call mom regularly	Have overcome financial difficulties

In putting together this matrix, you might find yourself getting stumped. That's okay. In fact, that's pretty typical. Because so many of us have spent so much of our time dwelling on the negative, we have a really hard time coming up with all the stuff that's great about us. We've locked it away and have decided it doesn't matter or doesn't warrant attention, so it may be hard to access.

If you are finding that's the case, the first thing you need to do is look out for your Sabby. They are probably trying very hard to keep you from accessing all the things that are great about you, because they know acknowledging your success makes you stronger and them weaker. Sabby's voice most commonly comes up as a "Yeah, but...." or a "That's no big deal." For example, you may think, "I donate my time to the local humane society every month." And Sabby may respond with, "Yeah, but you ONLY do it once a month and you have way more time than that!"

You see what Sabby is trying to do there? They're trying to take away your great thing by focusing on the negative. Sure, you could volunteer more. Everyone on the planet could volunteer more. It doesn't take away from the volunteering that you do participate in. It all has value, no matter what Sabby might say!

It might be helpful to involve someone else in this exercise (or multiple someone elses!). The people who know you best will certainly have awareness and insight into what's great about you, things that Sabby has blocked you from seeing. After all, they are choosing to be in your life for a reason, right? And asking different people may give you different answers. Your mom may have different feedback from your best friend or your spouse. It can be enlightening and valuable to hear what they have to say.

Get started on your matrix on page 115 and fill it up! And once you have completed it, I want you to post it somewhere where you can see it every day. Maybe on your bathroom mirror, your fridge, your nightstand, or even your coffeemaker. The idea is to see it every day to remind you what's great about you.

2. GIVE YOURSELF CREDIT

The next step in building your self-esteem is to focus on self-reinforcement—patting yourself on the back, so to speak. This is something that sometimes gets a bad rap, but most of us don't do nearly enough of it, even though it has so much value. In fact, most of us do the opposite by beating ourselves up for what we *didn't* do or what we did wrong. Usually this does nothing good for our motivation and gets us stuck in that cycle of negative thinking. What would really benefit us is focusing on the positive and really making ourselves feel good and accomplished for the things we've done well!

This concept is what I call *Identifying Your Wins*™. Wins are just something you've done well, something you've accomplished, something you are proud of. Wins can be anything that makes you feel good about yourself, or anything that you feel was the right thing to do. Let me give you some examples:

➡ I took an extra ten minutes this morning to make myself a delicious, healthy breakfast.

➡ I went out of my way to help a colleague at work.

➡ I called my mom today, even though I didn't feel like it.

➡ I felt I carried myself really well today.

➡ I am proud of myself for resisting the cookies in the breakroom.

➡ I'm pleased that I did the laundry instead of putting it off another day.

➡ Instead of giving in to cravings, I did something productive.

➡ I put all of my effort into my workout today.

➡ I put time aside to tackle my inbox today.

➡ I nurtured myself today and did something just for me.

➡ I only had one piece of bread at dinner.

Does this give you an idea about Identifying Your Wins? I'm guessing these are things you don't say to yourself very often—which is *exactly* why I want you to do it now.

Let's say we do one hundred things over the course of a day. We can do ninety-nine of those things right and one wrong, yet at the end of the day, all we are focused on is that one thing we did wrong (yup, dwelling on the negative again!). We should really be celebrating the massive list of things we've done right! Unfortunately, most of us are hard-wired to focus on the negative, especially when it comes to self-critique or self-assessment. This negative mode of thinking is a form of self-punishment that ultimately impedes our progress.

I want you to be on a mission to change this self-attack and start focusing on the positive instead of rejecting it. That starts with Identifying Your Wins regularly! Here's how you do it: Set an alarm on your phone to go off sometime midday—ideally between noon and 3 p.m.—and again at the end of your day, maybe around 9 or 10 p.m. When this alarm goes off, I want you to quickly think about your day so far and identify a win. Write it down on your wins list on page 116. Then, end of the day, identify another win and write that down as well.

Once again, you may find Sabby trying to interfere here. Sabby *loves* to talk you out of acknowledging your wins! Here are some examples of how Sabby might chime in:

➡️ You already acknowledged that win yesterday.

➡️ Yeah but you didn't do . . . .

➡️ That's no big deal. You should be doing that all the time anyway.

Here's the thing about Identifying Your Wins. It doesn't matter if it's something you've done before. It doesn't matter if it's something you've given yourself credit for before. It doesn't matter if you could have done more. And it doesn't matter if it's a "should." All that matters is that you've done it and you've given yourself credit for it. So when you hear Sabby chime in, fight back with logic and disengagement!

3. FIND YOUR SELF-AFFIRMING MANTRA

All of us have some areas where our self-esteem is weaker than in others. We could be really good at interpersonal things but terrible at work, or feel that we can achieve our goals in some areas but not others. We could manage anything that falls on our plate at work but not at home. We may be super-confident with public speaking and not at all with dating. We might need to concentrate more of our efforts in the areas where our self-esteem is weakest. And how do you figure out exactly what those areas may be? Well, Sabby can lead you right to them!

Let's look back to the previous chapters where we were tracking Sabby's behavior. As you may remember, there was some repetition to Sabby's voice, suggestions, and attacks. You may recall that Sabby likes to attack when they know they can win, hitting you right where you're the weakest or most vulnerable. Those are exactly the areas we need to work on. In reviewing the worksheet in Chapter 13, I want you to identify the area that Sabby addressed most frequently. This could be:

➡️ Your ability to tackle projects

➡️ Your ability to manage your weight

➡️ The idea that you will never succeed

➡️ The idea that you are always failing or are a failure

➡️ Your capabilities at work

➡️ Your attractiveness to others

➡️ The idea that your efforts won't matter

➡️ Your value to the world as a whole

Look through your Sabby's thoughts and see if you can find your weak or vulnerable point. Some of you may know it without even looking. That's good! Knowing is already half the battle! Once you've figured out your weak point, it's time to go back to the use of logic and develop a mantra that will truly shut Sabby down in this area and get you believing in yourself!

Let's imagine that Sabby is always attacking you for your follow-through, saying you never follow through on anything. To fight that, start brainstorming on *all* of the times in your life that you have followed through. Pull together a big list and look at the evidence that proves Sabby is wrong. And from that, you can pull together a powerful mantra. It could be, "I'm very good at following through" or "I've successfully followed through many, many times in my life." It's the truth, and it's rooted in fact and logic. You just have to start telling it to yourself!

Say Sabby always attacks your efforts in the dating world. They tell you no one will like you or no one will find you attractive. Okay, time to start evidence-gathering. Can you think of people who have found you attractive or liked you before? Refer back to your "Why I'm Great" Matrix for reminders about all of the reasons someone might like you.

From that, you can create a new mantra. Perhaps it's "I have lots of wonderful qualities and I will make a great partner," or "Many people have found me attractive in the past and more people will in the future," or "I'm a good person and very attractive and likeable." Again, the idea is to find the logic that you can relate to that will help you start battling this idea that Sabby has beaten into your brain!

Let's look at one more scenario. Perhaps Sabby is always hassling you about your ability to succeed in school or at work. Again, let's start digging through the evidence of all the times you've been successful in the past. If you're a student or have a job, it means you've succeeded at getting into school or getting a job. You could also look at the qualities you think are required to succeed and identify the ones that you have. Pull these ideas together into a new mantra. Something like "I'm fully capable of success and have already proven it," or "I've achieved success in the past and will continue to do so in the future."

Whatever your weak point is, here is the action plan:

➡ Identify it.

➡ Think about how Sabby attacks it.

➡ Gather evidence that proves Sabby wrong or fights them with logic.

➡ Turn that evidence into a mantra.

➡ Immerse yourself in that mantra.

And I mean really immerse yourself! Post that mantra everywhere! It could be on a sticky note on your bathroom mirror next to your "Why I'm Great" matrix—but I don't want you to stop there! Put it on your fridge, your nightstand, your computer, your phone home screen, your daily alarm in your phone, the ceiling above your bed, your desk, or your coffee table. Put it anywhere you look regularly or anywhere you might need a helpful reminder. And when you see the reminder, don't just look at it; read it! Take the ten seconds to actually read it, process it, and internalize it. *Believe it!* After all, it's based on logic and truth.

Use the next few worksheets to create your "Why I'm Great" matrix, track your wins throughout the week, and develop your self-affirming mantra!

☑ Why I'm Great Matrix

My Qualities	My Skills

My Behaviors	My Accomplishments

☑ Identifying My Wins

Date	Credit

☑ Finding My Self-Affirming Mantra

Identify Your Weak Point

Where does Sabby keep attacking? In what area do I have a hard time shutting Sabby down?

_____

_____

_____

_____

_____

_____

Specify How Sabby Attacks Your Weak Point

What does Sabby say or do to keep me weak in this area?

_____

_____

_____

_____

_____

_____

Gather Evidence That Proves Sabby Wrong

How do I know Sabby is wrong? What evidence refutes what Sabby keeps saying?

_____

_____

_____

_____

_____

_____

Create Your Self-Affirming Mantra

Use that evidence to create a strong statement that you can use anytime Sabby attacks this area in the future!

_____

_____

_____

_____

_____

_____

Chapter 17

SELF-CARE

"Withholding love is a form of self-sabotage, as what we withhold from others, we are withholding from ourselves."

—Marianne Williamson

It would be ridiculous of me to get through an entire book on fighting self-sabotage without addressing the role of self-care! At first glance, it might seem that these two concepts are not related, but when you take a closer look, you realize they are inextricably linked.

You've likely heard the self-care analogy of not being able to pour from an empty cup, meaning it's impossible to give if you are not taking care of yourself. We have also talked about your Sabby and how they like to overpower you and take control. Well, as you can imagine, it is a lot easier for Sabby to overpower you if you are weak or if your metaphorical cup is empty. That's where self-care comes into play.

Self-care comes in a variety of shapes and sizes. For some people, it means making sure they check their blood sugar regularly. For others, it means setting aside or "protecting" time for themselves so that the day isn't a haze of work, chores, and doing favors. Self-care can mean saying "no" when someone wants you to do something, but you need a break. Most people are super-busy nowadays. With that kind of go-go-go lifestyle, it can be easy to let things slip, and usually the things we do for ourselves are the first things to go.

Self-care should be customized to your life and your needs, wants, and habits. For instance, many of us really need to cut down on our screen time. We wake up, check our phone, read Facebook, watch the news as we get ready for our day, sit in front of a computer all day at work, come home and watch TV, and go to bed with our phones. Constantly filling up our brain space with stressful news, comparing ourselves to others on social media, or staring at a TV show instead of talking to our loved ones can directly and indirectly make us weaker and make Sabby seem stronger. And then we wake up the next morning, and the cycle starts all over again. In this example, reducing screen time can be a valuable act of self-care!

Sometimes, it can feel like your life is on hold until you conquer your goals. For example, you might put off creating a home or office environment that you love until you get that promotion. I mean, what's the point of having a beautiful home when you haven't achieved success yet? Well, have you ever walked into a room, a store, or a business and noticed your mood get a little brighter? You can thank any number of factors—natural light, warm colors, just the right amount of art, an impressively organized bookshelf, and so on.

In contrast, environments that are cluttered, dirty, and crowded can leave you feeling overwhelmed and without a single ounce of motivation to do anything. Ever. That's a doozy of an impact. And yet, it's not uncommon for people to tolerate clutter, to live out of boxes rather than finally unpacking them, and to accept a disorganized (and frustrating) office as a permanent part of their life. So you are actually holding off on doing something until you achieve a goal when it's that exact something that might help you achieve that goal!

And of course, the things we do for our bodies are equally as important: sleep, hydration, nourishing foods, regular mealtimes, and physical activity can all be part of a solid self-care plan. For example, exercising regularly may be an effective way to give yourself a break, help you think more clearly, and motivate you to continue pushing toward your goal. And in doing so, you feel stronger and more capable, which makes you better at fighting Sabby. Alternatively you may think, "I don't have time for a workout," so you power through your work and wear yourself out until you are completely mentally exhausted. Then when Sabby starts their attack, you have nothing left to fight them with!

Imagine a boxer getting ready for a big fight. For the week before, he gets very little sleep, eats a bunch of junk food, fills his schedule with a ton of stuff, and doesn't allow himself any time to decompress. How do you think he is going to do in the big fight? Probably not well at all, since he hasn't done any self-care that week! Now, imagine a boxer in the week before a big fight, who has been focused on self-care. They have slept and eaten well, removed burdens from their life, taken time out to decompress, and filled their free time with things that made them happy. This boxer is going to go into the fight feeling strong, capable, and empowered!

Clearly, taking good care of yourself is a critical part of ensuring you are in tip-top shape to fight your Sabby. So where do you need to focus when it comes to self-care? Let these questions guide you to create your own personal self-care plan:

➡ Do you often feel like you don't get enough sleep?

➡ Do you overload your body with processed foods and go without fruits and veggies often?

➡ Do you feel dehydrated or think you are not drinking enough water?

➡ Do you spend most of the day in front of a screen (phone, computer, TV, tablet)?

➡ Do you feel like there's never enough time in the day?

➡ Do you feel like you can never take time off for yourself?

➡ Does your calendar feel overwhelming?

➡ Do you struggle to say "no"?

➡ Do you wish you had more time for calming activities like baths, meditation, or reading?

➡ Do you find yourself wishing you had a day or night off?

If you answered yes to any (or many!) of these questions, then you need to focus on making some change in those areas. Use the questions to guide you into creating an action plan. If you feel that sleep is the primary issue, then commit to an action plan to get more sleep. If you struggle to say "no," identify areas where you can say "no" more often. Then let people close to you know that you're going to be saying "no" more often so they're not surprised and you don't feel as hindered to stay on track on your plan. Do what you need to do to take care of yourself and ensure you're in the best fighting shape to knock out Sabby!

> Take a few minutes out to create your personalized self-care plan on
> pages 122 to 123. Then plug your self-care goals into your calendar
> and make them as important as anything else you do each day!

✔ My Self-Care Plan

Make a plan for whatever area you feel you need to address below.

My plan to get more/better sleep:

_____

_____

My plan to put healthier foods in my body:

_____

_____

My plan to drink more water:

_____

_____

My plan to cut down on screen time:

_____

_____

My plan to open up time in my calendar:

_____

_____

My plan to incorporate me-time regularly:

_____

_____

_____

My plan to say "no" more:

_____

_____

_____

My plan to include more calming activities:

_____

_____

_____

My plan to take more time off:

_____

_____

_____

Chapter 18

ADDRESS YOUR DANGER ZONES

"We all have vulnerabilities that can sidetrack us from reaching our goals. Recognize the times when you're most likely to give into temptation, and make it harder for a single moment of weakness to sabotage your best efforts."

—Amy Morin

You've been fighting your Sabby, taking care of yourself, and building your self-esteem. All of that is wonderful and should be making you stronger and more powerful. But there may be a few areas you need to address that are very specific to you and just you! I like to call this concept *finding your danger zones.*

You might associate *the danger zone* with singer Kenny Loggins from the 1980s or with the animated television series *Archer*. But if you are a professional self-saboteur, chances are that you'll have a different understanding of this term. A self-sabotage danger zone is a situation that triggers you, making you feel like you've lost control of your behavior or your belief in your ability to change things; in other words, situations that automatically trigger your self-sabotaging behavior, situations where Sabby seems invincible.

The danger zone is a circumstance in which you are at significant risk of self-sabotage; a situation or environment where Sabby seems unbeatable. You might already be aware of your danger zones. But if you aren't, there are ways to figure out when and where you are most vulnerable.

Identify your own personal danger zone(s) by looking through all the hard work you've done so far in this workbook. You have identified areas where you are prone to self-sabotage, soft spots where Sabby likes to attack. And you've worked on fighting back in numerous different ways, all according to the plan. You've had lots of successes too, except . . .

Yes, that *except* area is your danger zone! Let me give you some examples.

DAVE

Dave's self-sabotage revolved around work, so he went through this book's program and made significant efforts to get around his self-defeating behavior. When Sabby told him that he was no good or he shouldn't bother with trying to get ahead, he successfully shut them down. He began putting in more effort at work because he started to believe in himself more and felt confident throughout his work day—except when it came to his counterpart at work, Hank.

Hank is exceptionally talented and makes all of his work look effortless. Dave would feel good until he had to present with Hank in the room. Dave started comparing himself to Hank all the time— comparisons that led him right back to the self-sabotaging behavior he'd worked so hard to get rid of. Hank is Dave's danger zone.

LISA

Lisa sabotaged herself when it came to eating. She had always been an on-again, off-again dieter and wanted to end the yo-yo cycle to stop her emotional eating. Lisa followed the program and made great strides to shut Sabby down when Sabby told her that she would always be an emotional eater or that she didn't deserve to hit her goals.

Lisa became much more in tune with her hunger and with how food made her feel, and her understanding helped her fight Sabby when they tried to convince her to give in to her cravings. She'd been doing great—except for when she went to her mother-in-law's house. Lisa went there for dinner once a week and, once she got there, she felt powerless against Sabby. She would snack mindlessly and extensively on junk food, massively overeat at dinner, and essentially throw in the towel. Lisa's mother-in-law's house is her danger zone.

DIANE

Despite wanting to find a partner, Diane had always been down on herself when it came to dating, so she shied away from online dating for fear that no one would message or go out with her. She went through the program and worked on her self-esteem to fight Sabby. Diane even joined some online dating programs and started chatting away with people.

She felt confident and even enjoyed it—except for when she had to meet someone in person. She canceled three dates at the last minute and essentially gave in when Sabby told her the person she was meeting wouldn't like her when they saw her in real life. Meeting a date for the first time is Diane's danger zone.

Are you getting a feel for this? Can you find your *except* situation? It could be something similar to one of the examples above: a specific person, an event or location, or a behavior. It could be a certain time of day, such as when you get home from work, or a circumstance, such as nights you are home alone. It could also be situational, such as when you have a tight deadline (or no deadline!).

Take some time to think through your successes in working through this program, and then identify where you are still getting stuck: your *except* situations. Write them down so we can develop an action plan to save you from your danger zones and give you your power back!

Counteracting danger zones can mean many different things. It can mean avoiding danger zones altogether if possible. (I mean, if we can avoid a stressful situation without repercussions, why not?) It can also mean developing healthy coping skills you can use when you encounter a danger zone so that it eventually becomes a not-so-dangerous zone. Protecting yourself from the danger zone can also mean planning an early escape from a situation that is making it hard for you to feel strong, competent, and in control.

The idea in developing an action plan is that you *expect* the behavior to occur; it is not something that catches you off-guard. By expecting it, you can know exactly what you are going to do in that situation so you don't have to think or make decisions; you just act.

Let me give you some examples of action plans based on the situations we just discussed.

Dave's danger zone was Hank at work. His action plan was as follows:

➡ He made a list of all the reasons he was as good as Hank (and sometimes better!) and put that list on his phone. He read it every morning before walking in to work and before he gave any presentations.

➡ When Dave gave presentations with Hank present, he would pick out someone on the opposite side of the room from Hank and essentially give the presentation to that person. This strategy kept Hank out of his line of sight and helped Dave, by focusing specifically on one person, to draw his energy and thoughts away from Hank.

➡ Dave actively tried to work with Hank more. He realized that he didn't know Hank very well and had made a lot of assumptions about him. Once he started working with him, he was able to take Hank off that pedestal by realizing he was just as flawed as the rest of us.

Lisa's danger zone was her mother-in-law's house. Her action plan was as follows:

➡ She made a plan to start going to her mother-in-law's house every other week, instead of weekly. She actually looked forward to having an extra night to herself and used it for self-care.

➡ Prior to going to her mother-in-law's house, Lisa created an eating plan that designated what she was going to eat while she was there, and how much. She told her husband her plan each week to keep herself accountable.

➡ She brought a veggie crudité each time that she could snack on instead of unhealthy foods.

➡ She made a plan to sit in a seat that was not within arm's reach of all the junk food on the table. She found when she was sitting close, she would mindlessly snack on everything, and being out of arm's reach changed this behavior considerably.

Diane's danger zone was meeting a first date in person. Her action plan was as follows:

➡ She kept a copy of her "Why I'm Great" matrix in her purse and spent five minutes reviewing it prior to a date.

➡ She engaged in opposite action when meeting a date and went into each situation fully expecting her dates to adore her.

➡ She played out the worst-case scenario of her date not being interested and wrote out reasons to engage regardless. She reminded herself that each date was an opportunity to "practice" dating, and that she might actually not like the person she was meeting, either.

Hopefully, those examples give you some good insight into how to approach these action plans. The idea is to focus on your fear or your knee-jerk reaction, then create plans to address it or impede it.

Now, it's your turn to develop and implement an action plan. Think through some ideas—you can have lots! If you are stuck, this is another example of a situation that may be useful to talk through with someone, as their perspective may give you different ideas. Run it by a friend, sibling, or spouse to see if they have suggestions that might be useful to try out. And remember, this is going to be a trial-and-error sort of thing. You may implement your action plan and find it needs tweaking or that some actions simply don't work. That's absolutely fine! Keep working on it and you will find your sweet spot!

Use the worksheet on pages 130 to 131 to write down your danger zone or zones and develop your action plan. Then start testing out your action plans!

✔ My Danger Zone Action Plan

Danger Zone #1 _____

Action Plan:

➡ _____

_____

➡ _____

_____

➡ _____

_____

➡ _____

_____

Danger Zone #2 _____

Action Plan:

➡ _____

_____

➡ _____

_____

➡ _____

_____

➡ _____

_____

Danger Zone #3 _____

Action Plan:

➡️ _____

_____

➡️ _____

_____

➡️ _____

_____

➡️ _____

_____

Chapter 19

MOVING FORWARD

"Your capacity expands in small increments each time you consciously let yourself enjoy the money you have, the love you feel, and the creativity you are expressing in the world. As that capacity for enjoyment expands, so does your financial abundance, the love you feel, and the creativity you express."

– Gay Hendricks

We've gone over what it's like to be trapped in the world of self-sabotage—it's not a great place to be. Thankfully, now we know what it's like to leave that all behind by identifying our Sabby, learning how to fight them, building ourselves up, and identifying and tackling our danger zones. And as we've been doing all of that, Sabby has gotten very quiet. But what if you stop paying attention and Sabby sneaks back in? Maybe you have a particularly bad day and Sabby takes advantage of that in order to regain some control. Then what?

Well, you just hop back on the wagon! Recovery from self-sabotaging behavior isn't without some bumps and challenges. Falling back into old patterns is to be expected. It does *not* mean the program isn't working—it just means that, as for a lot of people, breaking your habits sometimes includes two or three steps forward and one step back. When you're overcoming self-sabotage there's always a risk of panicking when the going gets tough and of going back to your old self-destructive behaviors. It makes sense—your old ways are what you know. And we've talked about the pull of that comfort zone! But realistically, if your old thought patterns have never worked for you to achieve your goals, they won't this time, either.

Instead, use your energy to recommit to this program. Remind yourself how much you actually want to achieve, how capable you are, and how the only thing standing in the way is that awful Sabby! Here are some tools you can use in the moment when you start questioning whether you should keep fighting or not:

➡ Remind yourself why you read this book in the first place. Maybe you picked this up because you have lost five, ten, or even fifteen years of your life to Sabby, or because you felt it was time to make a change. Perhaps you decided your goals and dreams were worth fighting for. Whatever it is, now is the time to remind yourself of what you want and where you are headed if you keep your focus.

➡ Be kind to yourself—extremely kind! Another habit that can be hard to break is the shame, guilt, and punishment that go along with self-sabotage. It's not uncommon for people to treat themselves badly for treating themselves badly! And that's a cycle that gets you nowhere. Treat yourself like you would a dear friend who was struggling. That might mean taking time to do something nice for yourself (a walk in the forest, a hot bath, a cappuccino), to ask a friend for support, or to go out of the way to make your day enjoyable. Whatever kindness is for you, you need to do that instead of trying to berate yourself into making a positive change. That doesn't work—millions have tried it! Slips happen. Perfection simply isn't part of this program.

➡ When the dust has settled, take some time to understand what triggered the return to self-sabotage. Were you overly stressed? Have you been getting enough sleep (honestly now, okay)? Are you overextended? Or was it just an old habit coming into play, as sometimes happens? Whatever the triggers were, take some time to think about how you can respond to them differently next time. Maybe you need to refocus on stress management. Should you rein in the late-night YouTube watching or Facebook posting, so you can get the sleep you need? Have you been telling yourself that you aren't as busy as you really are? Identify the situations that put you at risk of falling back into the self-sabotage routine, and do your best to stay far, far away from them. In other words, review your danger zones, determine whether there are any new ones that are catching you by surprise, and update your action plans.

➡ Add to your list of things you've learned. As you go through this program, you will discover all sorts of things about yourself. Whether it is identifying Sabby's form of attack, coming to know the danger zones that can send you back into old habits, or formulating the right balance of self-care and self-esteem building that can keep you headed in the right direction, you'll be surprised to see how much you've learned. But it is easy to forget all the progress you've made when you're struggling. By keeping track of all the learning and progress that has happened, you will have a powerful tool at your fingertips. You'll have the positives front and center, making it much harder for negative thinking to get in the way of sticking with the program.

➡ Make yourself a "first aid" kit of soothing items like candles, bath bombs, a favorite playlist, a foam roller, or whatever you like so they're waiting for you when you need them.

➡ Take the time to assess where you are and figure out what you need to do to get back on track. You can review items from My Check-In Checklist and from the list above, and dream up whatever else you can do to gently nudge yourself in the direction you want to go.

Review the My Check-In Checklist on page 136 monthly and make a
plan to keep yourself focused and on track moving forward!

✔️ My Check-In Checklist

	Am I doing this regularly?
Looking Out for Self-Sabotaging Behaviors	
Looking Out for Cognitive Distortions	
Fighting Sabby with Logic or Disengagement	
Fighting Sabby with Opposite Action	
Fighting Sabby with Systematic Desensitization	
Working on Confidence Building	
Addressing My Self-Care Needs	
Looking Out for Danger Zones	
Reminding Myself of My Goals	
Being Kind to Myself	

This month I will focus on the following:

_____

_____

I will use the following plan of attack:

_____

_____

_____

_____

Conclusion

My hope, at this point, is that you have made major changes in your life. Now, what?

Well, the hard part is done! If you have succeeded at everything in this book, you have done most of the heavy lifting. If you haven't, you can revisit the chapters that you haven't mastered yet, redo the worksheets, and continue to practice the included skills. Now, it's a matter of maintaining your success and directing it wherever you want to go. If you are happy with your changes and feel like they are moving you in a positive direction, then my only advice is *be patient*. As I've mentioned before, this is not a quick-change scheme. Slow and steady truly wins the race here. If you are making and maintaining all the changes outlined in this book, rest assured, they will have an impact!

If you want to continue the work you've started in this workbook, build your accountability, and connect with and support like-minded individuals, then I encourage you to join my Sabotage Warrior Coaching Program. This is an ongoing program that provides regular tips, tricks, and videos, including a monthly coaching call with me when we can focus directly on your needs, goals, or danger zones. It also includes a private Facebook group to connect with and gain support from others who are becoming Sabotage Warriors just like you!

If you want to make sure your self-sabotage stays a thing of the past, this coaching program is a great tool for you to achieve just that. It can bring you peace of mind and the satisfaction of knowing that you've turned your back on the self-sabotage that led you astray for so many years. It can be the beginning of a much happier, much healthier life. If you want company on your journey to a life that is free from self-sabotage, then my coaching program might be just the thing you're looking for.

Not sure if the online program is right for you? Feel free to drop me a line at dr.seti@meonlybetter. com. I'd be happy to discuss your situation with you and determine whether the program would be a good fit for your goals. In the meantime, I wish you all the best as you work toward freeing yourself from Sabby and becoming the ultimate Sabotage Warrior!

Here's to the new you!

Candice Seti

Acknowledgments

So many people came together to make this book possible.

First and foremost, I want to acknowledge everyone who gave me support during the writing process. Writing is not my forte and doesn't come easy to me. But I would describe myself as a helper and, as such, someone who wants to share my knowledge and expertise with everyone I can in an effort to help more people. For that reason, writing is an invaluable tool, and knowing that drives me to keep doing it. That being said, thank you to everyone who continually provided me with encouragement through the writing process. Every word of reinforcement, every "you can do it" or "keep at it" really helped keep me focused and motivated, and I am truly appreciative to those who provided ongoing support!

I am always appreciative and a little bit in awe of all my clients. It takes so much strength to reach out for help, and the therapeutic process, while arguably invaluable, can be difficult and trying. I so appreciate all of the efforts my clients have made, and continue to make, in therapy. It makes me feel wonderful to see all of your growth and forward movement, and I learn just a little bit more in my work with each and every one of you. Thank you for letting me accompany you on your journey and for trusting me to help get you where you need to go.

Thank you, Vivian Syroy, for being my first set of eyes on the original draft and helping me with expansion ideas. Your feedback was invaluable!

I would like to thank all of the copyeditors, artists, and publishers at Ulysses Press. And an extra special thanks to Ashten Evans for finding value in this topic and giving me the opportunity to present it to the world.

And finally, a perpetual thank you to my husband Matt for the endless support. Your belief in me is limitless, and I can't put into words how much it means to me to always have you in my corner.

About the Author

As a therapist, author, speaker, coach, and former yo-yo dieter, Dr. Candice Seti is committed to helping others achieve health and wellness while gaining self-confidence, stopping self-sabotage, and achieving their goals.

Dr. Seti maintains a very busy private practice in San Diego, California, where she works one-on-one with individuals, helping them understand their maladaptive behaviors and thought patterns while replacing them with a healthier perspective that allows them to overcome self-sabotage and thrive in their lives. She also offers services online, including video counseling and numerous do-it-yourself programs addressing weight loss, binge eating, insomnia, and specialty populations like PCOS and menopause.

Dr. Seti helps her patients understand their barriers and achieve success through behavioral lifestyle and cognitive changes. Her previous book, *Shatter the Yoyo*, provides readers with unique strategies, tips, and tricks on weight management that can be incorporated into a long-term healthy lifestyle instead of a short-term regimen that sets them up to regain weight.

Known as "The Weight-Loss Therapist" online, Dr. Seti is a licensed clinical psychologist, certified nutrition coach, certified weight management specialist, certified expert life coach, certified personal trainer, and certified insomnia treatment clinician. She is a featured contributor to numerous blogs, including *MyFitnessPal*, *Aaptiv*, and *Beachbody* and has appeared on FOX 32 Chicago, *Las Vegas Morning Blend*, *CBS 8 Morning Show*, NBC Palm Springs, and eHealth Radio Network.